To Billy
with love from
Helen
Xmas '11

Best wishes
Harry Upchard 15/11/11

What

PRESBYTERIANS
BELIEVE

by

The Very Rev. R.E.H. Uprichard
B.A., B.D., M.Th., Ph.D., D.D.

What Presbyterians Believe

Published by: The Oaks,
                51, Glebe Road, Ahoghill, BT42 2QW,
                Co. Antrim, Northern Ireland

e-mail: info@whatpresbyteriansbelieve.com

© The Oaks 2011. All rights reserved.

No part of this publication may be reproduced, stored in a retrieval system or transmitted, in any form, or by any means, electronic, mechanical, photocopying, recording or otherwise, without the prior permission of the publishers.

First published in a shorter form as "On Profession of Faith" by the Board of Evangelism and Christian Training, (Christian Training Committee) The Presbyterian Church in Ireland.

Edited and enlarged edition published 2011.

British Library Cataloguing in Publication Data available.

Paperback edition   ISBN: 978-0-9548784-0-5

Hardback edition   ISBN: 978-0-9548784-1-2

"Unless otherwise indicated, all Scripture quotations are from The Holy Bible, English Standard Version® (ESV®), copyright © 2001 by Crossway, a publishing ministry of Good News Publishers. Used by permission. All rights reserved."

Scripture quotations marked (NIV) are taken from the Holy Bible, New International Version®, NIV®. Copyright © 1973, 1978, 1984 by Biblica, Inc.™ Used by permission of Zondervan. All rights reserved worldwide. www.zondervan.com

Unless otherwise indicated quotations from The Westminster Confession and Catechisms in this publication are from The Westminster Confession and Catechisms in Modern English. Copyright © by Rowland S. Ward 1996, 2000, Special edition for distribution in Malawi – 2001, New Melbourne Press, 358, Mountain Hwy, Wantirna, Victoria, 3152, Australia. ISBN 0-9586241-4-3 All rights reserved.

Typesetting by The Oaks Secretarial Services, 02825878125

Front cover "After Harvest" in the Antrim countryside, outside the village of Ahoghill.

Printed and bound by CPI Group (UK) Ltd, Croydon, CR0 4YY

CONTENTS

Acknowledgements	ix
Foreword	xi
Introduction	xiii
God and You	xiii
Chapter 1	1
What God is Like	1
God is . . .	1
Powerful	1
Just	1
Good	2
Holy	2
Triune	3
God Speaks	4
Nature	4
Scripture	4
Son	6
God Acts	7
Creation	7
History	7
Salvation	8
Summary	9
God and You	9
What is God Like?	9
God is . . .	9
God is Powerful	9
God is Good	10
God is Holy	10
God Speaks	10
God Speaks Through Nature	10
God Speaks in Scripture	11
God Speaks in His Son	11
God Acts	12
God Acts in Creation	12
God Acts in History	12
God Acts in Salvation	13
Chapter 2	15
What Man is Like	15
Man's Potential	15
Original Potential	15
High Potential	16
Man's Problem	18

Basic Problem	18
Growing Problem	19
Inescapable Problem	21
Summary	23
What Man is Like	23
Man's Potential	23
Man's Problem	24

Chapter 3

God's Plan	25
Christ	26
Who He is	26
Divine	26
Works	26
Claims	27
Reputation	27
Human	28
Life	29
Impression	29
What He Did	30
Prophet	31
Priest	33
King	35
Conversion	37
God's Part - Regeneration	37
Sovereign	38
Necessary	38
Complete	39
Life-giving Word	39
Man's Part - Repentance and Faith	40
Repentance	41
Complete	41
Necessary	42
Faith	42
Come	44
Receive	44
Rely	45
Trust	45
Summary	47
God's Plan	47
Who Christ Is	47
What Christ Did	48
Christ as Prophet	48
Christ as Priest	48

Contents

Christ as King	49
Conversion	50
God's Side	50
Man's Side	50

Chapter 4 — 53

New Life	53
The New You	53
Justification	54
Adoption	55
Sanctification	56
Assurance	58
The Friends of the New Life	59
Word of God	60
Prayer	62
Fellowship	64
Summary	67
New Life	67
The New You	67
Justification	67
Adoption	67
Sanctification	68
Assurance	69
The Friends of the New Life	69
Word of God	69
Prayer	70
Fellowship	70

Chapter 5 — 71

Church	71
The Church and her Head	71
Vine	72
Body	73
Bride	74
Temple	75
People	77
The Presbyterian Church	79
Origin	79
Beliefs	80
Doctrine	81
Subordinate Standards	82
Government	83
Elder	83
Deacon	85
Presbyterian	86

Summary	88
Church	88
The Church and her Head	88
The Vine	88
The Body	88
The Bride	88
The Temple	88
People	89
The Presbyterian Church	89
Origin	89
Beliefs	89
Chapter 6	91
Sacraments	91
Baptism	94
Cleansing from Sin	94
Union with Christ	94
Admission to the Church	94
Covenant of Grace	95
Lord's Supper	99
Remembrance	99
Communion	99
Anticipation	100
Covenant of Grace	101
Communicant Membership	102
Summary	106
Sacraments	106
Baptism	106
The Lord's Supper	107
Communicant Membership	107
Chapter 7	109
Christian Life	109
Personal	109
Home	112
Courtship	113
Marriage	114
Parents	115
Children	116
Church	117
Faithfulness	117
Service	119
Fellowship	121
World	121
Work	122

Contents

Citizenship	123
Summary	126
Christian Life	126
Personal Life	126
Home Life	127
Church Life	128
Life in the World	128
Chapter 8	131
The Holy Spirit	131
Person	131
Work	135
Creation	135
Revelation	137
Redemption	142
Perseverance of the Saints	145
Assurance of Grace and Salvation	146
Summary	147
Holy Spirit	147
Person and Work	147
Creation	147
Revelation	147
Redemption	148
Chapter 9	149
The Last Things	149
The Second Coming	149
The Gathering of God's People	152
The Signs of the Second Coming	153
The calling of the Gentiles	154
The conversion of Israel	154
The Great Apostasy and the Great Tribulation	154
The Coming of Antichrist	155
Signs and Wonders	155
The Millennium	156
Premillennialism	157
Postmillennialism	157
Amillennialism	157
Judgement	159
Death and Beyond	159
Death for the Believer	160
Death for the Unbeliever	161
Life after Death	162
Summary	163

    The Last Things 163
Chapter 10 165
  Covenant 165
    Introduced 165
    Initiated 166
    Confirmed 167
    Foretold 167
    Explained 168
    Fulfilled 169
    Applied 170

  Summary 173
    Covenant 173

Chapter 11 175
  The Bible 175
    Inspired 175
    Accurate 178
    Sufficient 179

  Summary 183
    The Bible 183

Chapter 12 185
  Worship 185
    Meaning of Worship 185
    Modes of Worship 185
      Old Testament 185
        Individual Worship 185
        Covenant Worship 186
        Sacrificial Worship 186
      New Testament 188
        Fulfilment 188
        Continuity 190
    Mandate for Worship 196
    Matters of Worship 200
      Attitude 200
      Activities 201
      Music 202

  Summary 205
    Worship 205

For Further Reading 207

ACKNOWLEDGEMENTS

We would like to proffer our indebtedness to the Very Rev. Dr R.E.H. Uprichard for allowing us to publish such a fine work. His study and expertise in these subjects are invigorating.

He has given of his time and expertise to put together a work, which will profit anyone to understand these doctrines as laid out in scripture and whet their appetite for further study of God's word.

We would like to thank all who have contributed in any manner. We do apologise for not mentioning individuals by name, but there are so many to thank for their help, encouragement and support in this project; their comments, proof-reading and suggestions have been invaluable.

We also offer our thanks and gratitude to the Presbyterian Congregation of Trinity, Ahoghill, for the substantial gift, which has greatly helped towards the printing of this book.

We are grateful also to those who are involved in the translation of this volume as it is our intention to have it printed in Chechewa and Tumbuka, two main languages spoken, in Malawi, Central Africa.

FOREWORD

This book which contains twelve chapters on important topics of the Christian faith, is intended for use as a course of instruction for those preparing to come to the sacrament of the Lord's Supper. It may also be used to help others to know what the Presbyterian Church believes the Word of God to teach on these subjects.

In the manual variations of type are used to indicate several sources of quotations. When Scripture is quoted italicised type is used as follows:-

"The Lord saw that the wickedness of man was great in the earth, and that every intention of the thoughts of his heart was only evil continually" (Genesis 6:5).

Another major source of quotation is the Shorter and Larger Catechisms and these are indicated by the following examples of type:-

"The decrees of God are his eternal plan, according to the purpose of his will, by which, for his own glory, he has foreordained what ever comes to pass; [yet in such a manner as to be in no way the author of sin]" (S.C. 7).

"The work of creation is the work God did in the beginning by his powerful word and for himself, when he made of nothing the world and all things in it, within the space of six days, and all very good" (L.C. 15).

It is suggested that the material be studied in class-groups and the worksheets completed by each individual as a follow-up exercise.

Remember, do not just read and do the exercises. Apply them to your life.

"Do not merely listen to the word and so deceive yourselves. Do what it says" (James 1:22).

INTRODUCTION

GOD AND YOU

What, then, is a Christian? A Christian is someone who has a personal relationship with God. The Shorter Catechism describes the purpose of this relationship as being to *"glorify God, and to enjoy him for ever"* (S.C. 1). And, therefore, we must turn to the Bible to find out what it teaches about the nature of God and of man. People say, *"I believe in God"*. They usually mean they believe in God's existence. This says very little since the Bible reminds us that demons or evil spirits also believe (James 2:19). It all depends on what kind of god they believe in and how they believe in him.

For some, God is like a great Father Christmas, good and kind, who gives them what they want and overlooks their faults. For others, God is like a heavenly policeman watching all the time, ready to pounce on them in judgment when they do wrong. The Shorter Catechism presents a proper idea of God, teaching how to believe in him. There is only one standard.

> *"The word of God, which consists of the Scriptures of the Old and New Testaments, is the only rule to direct us how to glorify and enjoy him"* (S.C. 2).

CHAPTER 1

WHAT GOD IS LIKE

What picture of God does the Bible present? The Bible has many things to say about God but three aspects are especially important.

GOD IS . . .

Many discussions about religion begin with an attempt to deduce the existence of God by human reasoning by so-called *"philosophical"* proofs. In total contrast, the Bible simply accepts the reality of God going on from that to explain what God is like.

POWERFUL

The Bible depicts God as mighty, indeed almighty, all-powerful, sovereign. He has all power and is in complete control of every situation. He is the creator of all things who never grows tired or weary. He is in command of all things in heaven and on earth, the king of kings ruling all leaders and peoples. He is the source of all life and sustains everything by his power. Nothing is too difficult or impossible for him.

JUST

The Bible also describes God's moral character. The psalmist makes the statement,

> *"Righteous are you, O Lord, and right are your rules"* (Psalm 119:137).

Clearly expecting the answer "yes", Abraham asks,

> *"Shall not the Judge of all the earth do what is just?"* (Genesis 18:25).

The word "righteous" means "straight" as opposed to

"twisted" or "crooked". We know the difficulties we can get into dealing with a crooked businessman. God is straight. He acts in complete consistency with his perfect justice. He is just to all men. We can depend on his uprightness.

GOOD

God is good in the sense of being kind. He not only created all things but provides for his creation. He preserves both man and animals, providing fruitful harvests and food in due course for all people whether they are good or evil. In a remarkable statement the Bible teaches that this is a central feature of God's character: *"God is love"* (I John 4:8,16). However, God cares not only for man's body, but shows the highest form of his care through his concern for man's soul.

HOLY

The word holy means "cut off", "separate", "apart". When the Bible describes God as holy, it usually has two things in view. **First**, it teaches that God is separate from us as a creator is separate from the creature. He is spirit, we are flesh. He has made us, we are dependent on him. **Secondly**, the Bible also reminds us that God is separate from us in character. He is righteous, we are twisted. He is good, we are evil. The prophet Habakkuk, distressed about the prevailing wickedness in his day pleads with God in these terms:

> *"You who are of purer eyes than to see evil and cannot look at wrong . . ."* (Habakkuk 1:13).

For Habakkuk, God was holy in the sense of being morally pure and sinless. God is separate from sin.

The Bible says many other things about God's character. The Shorter Catechism gives a full list of them.

> *"God is a Spirit, infinite, eternal and unchangeable in his being, wisdom, power, holiness, justice, goodness and truth"* (S.C. 4).

But we have studied enough to show how great and good God is but are left with a problem. Since God is holy and sinless, and we are impure and sinful, our relationship with and knowledge of God is hindered. Sin creates a barrier between us and God. We will return to this problem later.

TRIUNE

The Bible teaches that God is one and yet more than one. God is one in the sense of being the only God. There are no other gods. God is also one in the sense of being a unity. Yet within this unity there is a plurality, a plurality which does not harm God's unity. The Shorter Catechism describes it like this:

> *"There are three persons in the Godhead: the Father, the Son and the Holy Spirit; and these three are one God, the same in substance, equal in power and glory"* (S.C. 6).

We call this unity and plurality the triune being of God. God is a trinity. The Old Testament contains only hints of the trinity, which is presented more clearly in the New Testament. Yet even in the New Testament it is not taught as explicitly as some other aspects of God's nature, not because this view of God is unimportant but because it was totally accepted and believed by the first Christians. For them, Jesus was God and the Holy Spirit was God, just as the Father was God.

The doctrine of this trinity is affirmed at the beginning of Jesus' ministry in his baptism. God the Father states that Jesus is his Son. God the Son is anointed through his baptism as Saviour, as he identifies with sinful man. God the Spirit confirms this by descending in the form of a dove. We hear it at the close of Jesus' ministry in the final instructions which he gave his followers,

> *"Go therefore and make disciples of all nations, baptizing them in the name of the Father and of the Son and of the Holy Spirit"* (Matthew 28:19).

We find, too, it in Jesus' teaching. Jesus claims,

> *"I and the Father are one"* (John 10:30).

Jesus promises,

> *"And I will ask the Father, and he will give you another Helper, to be with you forever, even the Spirit of truth, whom the world cannot receive, because it neither sees him nor knows him. You know him, for he dwells with you and will be in you"* (John 14:16, 17).

GOD SPEAKS

The God of the Bible speaks, a creator who communicates with his creation. He reveals himself to us. His revelation of himself to us is one way in which the God of the Christian faith is unique, whereas the god of many other religions, even if he is regarded as creator, has no interest at all in his creation. The thrilling thing about our God is that he has something to say to us.

How does God speak? The Bible teaches three ways in which God speaks to us through: Nature, Scripture, and the Son.

NATURE

God discloses his greatness to us through the world around us. The psalmist says,

> *"The heavens declare the glory of God, and the sky above proclaims his handiwork"* (Psalm 19:1).

When Paul was seeking to persuade the Roman Christians that pagans were guilty before God, he wrote that God's eternal power and divine nature were clearly seen, being understood from what God had made (Romans 1:20). Nature is not the most forceful way by which God speaks to us, but it is, nevertheless, one way, a silent, visual witness to God's greatness and power.

SCRIPTURE

God speaks much more clearly through scripture. God did this in a variety of ways in Old Testament days. He spoke through visions and dreams to patriarch and prophet. He addressed his people through prophet, priest and wise man. And eventually, all of this was committed to writing and forms the Old Testament scripture, for scripture means something written down. Jesus reminds us of the three divisions in Old Testament scripture - the Law, the Prophets and the Psalms or Writings,

> *"Then he said to them, 'These are my words that I spoke to you while I was still with you, that everything written about me in the Law of Moses and the Prophets and the Psalms must be fulfilled'"*
> (Luke 24:44).

The New Testament writers underline the importance of scripture as the means of hearing what God says. Paul claims that all scripture is inspired, – indeed, expired would be better. The word means, **"God-breathed"**,

> *"All Scripture is breathed out by God and profitable for teaching, for reproof, for correction, and for training in righteousness, that the man of God may be competent, equipped for every good work"*
> (II Timothy 3:16, 17).

The words of scripture are the very Word of God. For this reason, Paul explains, they help us to find forgiveness of sin and to grow in the Christian life. Peter says that the prophets were guided by God's Spirit in what they spoke and wrote, – just as a sailing boat is carried on course directly to its destination by a strong wind. Indeed, Peter teaches that Paul's letters are scripture,

> *". . . just as our beloved brother Paul also wrote to you according to the wisdom given him, as he does in all his letters when he speaks in them of these matters. There are some things in them that are hard to understand, which the ignorant and unstable twist to their own destruction, as they do the other Scriptures"* (II Peter 3:15, 16).

This doctrine is very important. It means that God spoke through inspired writings in both Old and New Testaments.

Prophets and apostles combine to give us God's very own words. This is why the Shorter Catechism teaches that it is the Word of God "contained in the scriptures of the Old and New Testaments" which is the only rule to direct us in getting to know and love God. The Shorter Catechism also stresses the importance of what scripture teaches.

> *"The Scriptures principally teach what man is to believe concerning God, and what duty God requires of man"* (S.C. 3).

SON

God not only speaks to us through scripture, he addresses us through his Son. It is one thing to read a book about a subject, however well written. It is something quite different to listen to a teacher, who is full of excitement about his subject or to meet a person, for whom that subject is really alive. God speaks to us personally through Jesus Christ.

John explains in his gospel how Jesus is God's complete Word to us.

> *"And the Word became flesh and dwelt among us, and we have seen his glory, glory as of the only Son from the Father, full of grace and truth"* (John 1:14).

There can be no clearer view of God than that which we have in Jesus, in whom we see all God's glory. The writer to the Hebrews reminds us that Jesus is God's final Word to us.

> *"Long ago, at many times and in many ways, God spoke to our fathers by the prophets, but in these last days he has spoken to us by his Son, . . ."* (Hebrews 1:1, 2).

This does not mean that there is a conflict between God speaking through scripture and God speaking through his Son. The two, rather, complement one another. God speaks to us about his Son, the living Word, through scripture, his written Word.

What God is Like

GOD ACTS

The God of the Bible is a God who acts, totally in contrast to the so-called gods of the ancient world or of other religions. Not only are many of these gods seen as uninterested in their worshippers, but completely inactive. Even if they are regarded as creator gods, they abandon the world they have made to its own devices.

The God of the Bible is different. Constantly seen as active and involved in the world he has made, God's acts back up his words. These activities fall into three main groups: creation, history, and salvation.

CREATION

The Shorter Catechism gives a grand summary of the Bible story of creation.

> *"The work of creation is the making by God of all things from nothing, by his powerful word, in the space of six days, and all very good"* (S.C. 9).

The Bible goes on to teach how God did not abandon his perfect creation but cares, provides and continues so to do.

HISTORY

God is also active in history. Many of the books of the Bible are historical in that they record God's activities in his world. The Old Testament tells how God chose a people as his own, gave them a land to live in and a law to live by, provided kings to rule over them and prophets to guide them, protecting and helping them throughout their generations. The New Testament shows God sending his Son and how, through his Son's life, death and resurrection, God called a people to be his own guiding and helping them through teachers and leaders. None of this happened by chance, but indeed through God's constant control of his world. The Shorter Catechism sums it up like this:

> *"The decrees of God are his eternal plan, according to the purpose of his will, by which, for*

his own glory, he has foreordained whatever comes to pass; [yet in such a manner as to be in no way the author of sin]" (S.C. 7).

SALVATION

As we have seen, God is active in creation and in history. And for a particular reason. When we study the way God created man and the way he controlled history, a deeper plan comes to view. For example, God chose Abraham and his descendants not just to do them good but that eventually, from their nation, one would be born who would do good, not only to Jews, but Gentiles as well.

This leads us to the climax of God's activities in sending his Son, Jesus Christ. The Bible tells us that God sent his Son into the world so that man might escape God's judgment, have everlasting life, be redeemed or released from the slavery of evil, and be saved from his sin. God was active in creation and history so that, above all, he might be active in salvation.

The God of the Bible, then, is a God who is powerful, just and good. We can depend on him. He is also holy. So we must fear him and consider the problem of our sin and how sin hinders our relationship with him. God speaks to us. We must listen to him. God is active towards us. We must respond to him.

What God is Like

SUMMARY

GOD AND YOU

WHAT IS GOD LIKE?

GOD IS . . .

This section of the book mentions four characteristics, or attributes, of God - His power, justice, goodness and holiness.

1. Work out from the following references which of the characteristics the writer has in mind. Write each one alongside the reference.

Isaiah 6:3	God is	
Daniel 4:37	God is	
Exodus 15:6	God is	
Psalm 100:5	God is	

In each of the four questions below use the appropriate references from Question 1. You will need to look at the whole passage in which the reference is placed.

GOD IS POWERFUL

2. What was the special event that caused Moses and the Israelites to sing their song of praise to God?

_____

_____

_____

9

3. Mention some of the ways in which God's power was displayed throughout this event.

_____

_____

_____

GOD IS GOOD

4. List the other attributes of God that are mentioned alongside his goodness.

_____

_____

_____

GOD IS HOLY

5. What was the reaction of the person who experienced a revelation of the holiness of God?

_____

_____

_____

GOD SPEAKS

GOD SPEAKS THROUGH NATURE

1. Study Psalm 19:1-6. It speaks of God's revelation of himself in nature, while the remaining verses emphasise God's fuller revelation of his purposes in the laws which he gave his people.

What God is Like

What do you think we can learn about him from the revelation in nature?

_____

_____

_____

GOD SPEAKS IN SCRIPTURE

2. God speaks much more clearly through Scripture. Look up II Timothy 3:15-17. The Greek word translated "inspired" or "God-breathed" is theopneustos. It literally means God "expired" or "breathed out" his Word. From this passage write down the effect of the Scriptures upon Timothy. You should be able to find five or six.

    _____

    _____

    _____

3. Look up II Peter 1:20-21. If someone said to you that the Bible writers were simply expressing their own thoughts and ideas about God, how would this passage help you answer that?

    _____

    _____

    _____

GOD SPEAKS IN HIS SON

4. It has been said that if you want to know what God is like, look at Jesus Christ. Christians believe that Jesus is an image or mirror of God. Look up John 1:1-2 and also verse 14 and write in your own words what these verses tell us about Jesus.

    _____

_____

_____

GOD ACTS

God has been described as being like a clock maker. That means he made the world and now leaves it to *"keep ticking"* and eventually to stop. That illustration describes a God who, having created the world has no longer any involvement in it. This is not the way the Bible describes God. Rather, he is not only the God who creates but who also is involved in the world he has made.

GOD ACTS IN CREATION

1. Read Genesis 1. What phrase keeps recording, like a repeated chorus? **See verses 10, 12, 18, 21, 25.**

   _____

   _____

2. What does this tell us about the world?

   _____

   _____

GOD ACTS IN HISTORY

3. Some of the Old Testament books are poetry, others are prophetic, while others are records of historical events.
   e.g. (a) What significant historical event is recorded in Exodus?

   _____

   _____

What God is Like

4.   e.g. (b) What significant historical event is recorded in Nehemiah (chapter 1)?

_____

_____

GOD ACTS IN SALVATION

5.   This, in a nutshell, is what God's activity is about. Here are some people who spoke of God's salvation. Match the correct verse to the person.

Exodus 15:1-2	David	
Luke 1:69	Peter	
I Chronicles 16:23	Moses	
Luke 2:30	Simeon	
Acts 4:12	Zechariah	

CHAPTER 2

WHAT MAN IS LIKE

MAN'S POTENTIAL

The picture, of God's character, which the Bible presents is marked by evenness, stability and perfection. By contrast, man as portrayed in the Bible is very different. At times he is capable of reaching great heights, but on other occasions, sinks to great depths of evil and treachery. Moreover, there is a contrast between man before he fell into sin, a creature of amazing and exciting potential, and man after he had sinned, a creature faced by an insoluble problem. This is our theme as we study man in the Bible.

ORIGINAL POTENTIAL

Man's potential is evident from the very beginning of the Bible story. It is clear from the way in which he was created. The creation of man was special, he was uniquely made. In Genesis 1 the creation is introduced by the frequently repeated phrase *"And God said, 'Let there be . . .'"* and it was so (Genesis 1:3, 6, 9, 11, 14, 20, 24). Man is creation, however, is described differently. God's command, *"Let us make man"* (Genesis 1:26), is much more personal, a special act of creation by the triune God compared with the somewhat impersonal calling into existence of his earlier acts of creation. This command of God suggests that he took a special interest in forming this species of creature, the crown and climax, indeed, of his creation.

This impression of man's uniqueness arises also in Genesis 2, where everything God makes is made for man's benefit. God places man in a garden which he has planted for him, full of a variety of trees, good both in appearance and for food. God commands man to work the garden purposefully and gives man a wide range of freedom in it. God brings the animals to man for him to name and thus show his authority over them. God provides man with a companion to share life with him. The very detail of God's personal and intimate creation of man compared with the creation of vegetation and animal life further stresses man's superiority.

> *"then the Lord God formed the man of dust from the ground and breathed into his nostrils the breath of life, and the man became a living creature"* (Genesis 2:7 cf 2:9, 19).

These features, therefore, emphasise how different and unique was the creation of man among all the other forms of creation, reminding us not only of God's special interest in man but also of his love and care for him.

> *"God who made the earth*
> *The air, the sky, the sea*
> *Who gave the light its birth*
> *Careth for me"*
> (Sarah Betts Rhodes)

Man is the special object of God's creation and providence. Providing him with great dignity as a creature, we must therefore, guard against anything which robs man of that dignity.

The Bible's description of man's creation stresses man's higher intelligence over the animal world. Since man was given the ability to think reflectively, to be creative and to enjoy purposeful work we must promote a society in which he may freely do these things.

These gifts of God imposed on man, of course, certain weighty responsibilities. It requires of man responsible management. Man's lordship over the world demands his interest in, and care for, the world which God has provided for him. God has given man a good environment to live in. Man must care for it as God cared for him.

HIGH POTENTIAL

The greatest and most profound potential of mankind,

however, is evident in the fact that he has been created in the image of God.

> *"Then God said, 'Let us make man in our image, after our likeness. And let them have dominion over the fish of the sea and over the birds of the heavens and over the livestock and over all the earth and over every creeping thing that creeps on the earth.' So God created man in his own image, in the image of God he created him; male and female he created them"* (Genesis 1:26, 27).

What does the Bible mean by saying that man was created in the image or likeness of God? There is little difference in meaning between the words "image" and "likeness", which they are simply saying, that there is a link between man and God, not evident in any other of God's creatures. A number of explanations have been suggested.

Some have thought of a kind of physical link, the upright and erect stance of man in a world where the majority of creatures are "on all fours".

Some have stressed man's ability to think and reason, to reflect and communicate in speech and writing, with an intelligence superior to the animal world. Others have emphasised man's lordship over creation as the unique image of God in man.

For many, however, these three explanations fail to convey the full meaning of man's creation in God's image. They see rather a spiritual connection between man and God as the real link, evident in man's ability to talk to God and listen to what God says to him. Man is placed in a totally good environment and able to work purposefully and enjoyably in it. Evil had no part either in him or in his surroundings. Before he sinned, man was morally good and perfect, as God had made him.

Placed alongside this Old Testament teaching, two remarks made by Paul in his New Testament letters, confirm this moral explanation of the image. Describing how God's salvation changes a person, Paul declares that it restores the fallen image of God in man. Paul tells the Colossian Christians that they have,

> *"and have put on the new self, which is being renewed in knowledge after the image of its creator"* (Colossians 3:10).

He urges the Ephesian Christians

> *". . . to put on the new self, created after the likeness of God in true righteousness and holiness"* (Ephesians 4:24).

The initial and high potential which mankind had as created by God is truly remarkable, highlighting more clearly the disastrous effect of sin on mankind which is the next part of our study. The Shorter Catechism includes an excellent summary of man's potential as God had created him.

> "God created man, male and female, in his own image, in knowledge, righteousness and holiness, with rule over the creatures" (S.C. 10).

MAN'S PROBLEM

Man's great potential was shattered by the Fall. We use the word "Fall" to describe what happened to Adam and Eve. When they sinned, they "fell" from the good and perfect condition of knowledge, righteousness and holiness, in which God had made them, into a state of turmoil, confusion and evil. Behind the Fall was sin. As we study how Adam and Eve fell and the results that came from the Fall, we learn some sombre lessons about sin and what it does to us.

BASIC PROBLEM

God permitted Adam and Eve to eat the fruit of all the trees in the garden except that of the tree of knowledge of good and evil. When they ate the fruit of that tree they disobeyed God by breaking God's law.

This event helps us understand the subtlety of the devil in

tempting us to disobey God. As he spoke to Eve, the devil questioned God's Word, denied its truth and then maligned God, attributing evil motives to him (Genesis 3:1, 4, 5). Eve listened, looked, lingered, and then gave to Adam to eat as well (Genesis 3:6). Their disobedience was sin and what happened to Adam and Eve happens to us daily in thought, word and deed. It is "second nature" to us.

Sin is second nature to us not just because we can trace what happened to Adam and Eve in our lives daily, but because what happened to Adam and Eve then affects us now. The Fall of our first parents is basic in that its results are evident in the kind of people we are today. We are sinners. We have a nature prone to listen to the devil and to disobey God.

Paul explains this as he writes to the Christians at Rome.

> *"Therefore, just as sin came into the world through one man, and death through sin, and so death spread to all men because all sinned"* (Romans 5:12).

The Shorter Catechism puts it in this way.

> *"Since the covenant of life was made with Adam for his descendants as well as for himself, all mankind descending from him in the ordinary manner, sinned in him, and fell with him in his first transgression"* (S.C. 16).

This stresses the seriousness of man's basic problem of sin. It is part of his make-up, his fallen nature. He is born a sinner. This aspect of sin is called *"Original Sin"* (S.C. 18).

GROWING PROBLEM

Another problem about sin is that it grows and spreads within human nature, another truth clearly seen in the Genesis story. A study of Genesis 4:1 to 6:7 as a unit will teach the growth and spread of sin throughout mankind.

> *"Cain spoke to Abel his brother. And when they were in the field, Cain rose up against his brother Abel and killed him. Then the Lord said to Cain,*

> *'Where is Abel your brother?' He said, 'I do not know; am I my brother's keeper?'*
>
> *And the Lord said, 'What have you done? The voice of your brother's blood is crying to me from the ground. And now you are cursed from the ground, which has opened its mouth to receive your brother's blood from your hand. When you work the ground, it shall no longer yield to you its strength. You shall be a fugitive and a wanderer on the earth.'*
>
> *Cain said to the Lord, 'My punishment is greater than I can bear. Behold, you have driven me today away from the ground, and from your face I shall be hidden. I shall be a fugitive and a wanderer on the earth, and whoever finds me will kill me."*
>
> *Then the Lord said to him, 'Not so! If anyone kills Cain, vengeance shall be taken on him sevenfold.' And the Lord put a mark on Cain, lest any who found him should attack him.*
>
> *Then Cain went away from the presence of the Lord and settled in the land of Nod, east of Eden"* (Genesis 4:8-16).
>
> *"And Lamech took two wives. The name of the one was Adah, and the name of the other Zillah. Adah bore Jabal; he was the father of those who dwell in tents and have livestock. His brother's name was Jubal; he was the father of all those who play the lyre and pipe"* (Genesis 4:19-21).
>
> *"Lamech said to his wives: 'Adah and Zillah, hear my voice; you wives of Lamech, listen to what I say: I have killed a man for wounding me, a young man for striking me'""* (Genesis 4:23).

One writer describes it like this. "The immediate sequel in the unfolding history of Adam's family is the catalogue of sins:- envy, malice, hatred, homicide, polygamy, and violence". The climax of this process comes in Genesis 6:5,

What Man is Like

> *"The Lord saw that the wickedness of man was great in the earth, and that every intention of the thoughts of his heart was only evil continually"* (Genesis 6:5).

So sin is instinctive, universal and continual in man's nature. It has reached mammoth proportions.

> *"Now the earth was corrupt in God's sight, and the earth was filled with violence. And God saw the earth, and behold, it was corrupt, for all flesh had corrupted their way on the earth"* (Genesis 6:11, 12).

We use the phrase "Total Depravity" to describe the result of this growth of sin. Total depravity does not mean that every person is as bad as he could be, rather that, but for God's grace he would be. Every part of man, his thinking, emotions, will and actions is corrupted by sin.

The Shorter Catechism describes total depravity as follows:

> *"The sinfulness of the state into which man fell includes the guilt of Adam's first sin, the lack of the righteousness which he had at first, and the corruption of every part of his nature, which is commonly called Original Sin, together with all actual sins which flow from it"* (S.C. 18).

The Apostle James gives a vivid picture of the birth and growth of sin.

> *"But each person is tempted when he is lured and enticed by his own desire. Then desire when it has conceived gives birth to sin, and sin when it is fully grown brings forth death"* (James 1:14, 15).

Sin is like a moral cancer, which spreads throughout our entire human nature, destroying us and separating us from God.

INESCAPABLE PROBLEM

Perhaps the worst thing about sin in man's nature is that it is humanly speaking, inscapable. It affects not only man's relationship with God in this life, separating him from God but also resulting in eternal punishment after death.

Genesis 3 tells how, because of sin, the serpent, Adam, Eve and the earth itself came under the punishment or curse of God, so that ultimately as a result of sin, man was banished from the Garden of Eden (Genesis 3:23). After the Flood the same result of separation from God and death's judgment came upon all mankind (Genesis 6:6, 7). Sin inevitably brings death to mankind and separation from God.

One of the most gripping descriptions of what sin does to us in this life, anticipating also its effects in the life to come, is given by Paul writing to the Ephesians. Because of sin, man is dead to God,

> *"And you were dead in the trespasses and sins"* (Ephesians 2:1).

He is disobedient toward God,

> *"the spirit that is now at work in the sons of disobedience—"* (Ephesians 2:2).

Above all, he is in danger of eternal punishment

> *"by nature children of wrath"* (Ephesians 2:3).

The Shorter Catechism is equally clear about the ultimate results of sin in our nature,

> "The fall brought upon mankind loss of communion with God, and his wrath and curse, so that we are justly liable to all miseries in this life, to death itself, and to punishment in hell for ever" (S.C. 19).

Man, on his own, is unable to deal with the problem of sin, a problem basic to his nature. He is born with it, it grows in him spreading through him as the years pass. He cannot cope with it or control it. Eventually, it destroys his body and separates him eternally from God.

When we recall the way in which God had first created him, full of potential and hope, in knowledge, righteousness and holiness with dominion over the creatures, man's plight is all the more tragic.

Gladly the solution to man's problem of sin is the key theme of the Bible - **the story of salvation or deliverance.** To that we now turn.

SUMMARY

WHAT MAN IS LIKE

MAN'S POTENTIAL

1. "What is man?" asked the Psalmist long ago (Psalm 8:4). One answer is that God created mankind with great potential. Look at these verses from Genesis 1:4, 14, 15 and 25. Now, look at vv26, 27 and write down your answers to this question.

   _____

2. What are the differences in the description of God's creation of man and the other parts of creation?

   _____

   _____

   Reference has been made to Psalm 8. From this Psalm write down what is written there about man's potential, under the following headings:-

3. Man's relationship with God

   _____

   _____

4. Man's relationship with the rest of Creation

MAN'S PROBLEM

1. Sin is the tendency we all have to do wrong. Even when I know what is right, something inside me makes me want to do wrong. How does Paul put it in Romans 7:18, 19?

2. Isaiah, uses the illustration of sheep to describe mankind. In what ways are people like sheep? Look up Isaiah 53:6.

3. Sin is a growing problem. Like weeds in a garden they grow and spread. This is clearly seen in the Genesis story. For example look at Genesis 4. What specific sins can you discover in the relationship between Cain and Abel in vv 1-8?

4. Sin is the inescapable problem in that it separates us from God, unless dealt with. What does Romans 6:23 say about the final result of our sin?

CHAPTER 3

GOD'S PLAN

It is intriguing to see how God dealt with the problem of man's sin. God solved the problem in his plan of salvation. The Shorter Catechism gives a marvellous description of this plan.

> *"God, solely of his love and mercy, from all eternity elected some to everlasting life, and entered into a covenant of grace to deliver them out of the state of sin and misery, and to bring them into a state of salvation by a Redeemer"* (S.C.20).

"Covenant of grace" is an important term in that description. What is a covenant of grace? It is a promise of God's undeserved favour. The Old Testament has much to say about God's covenant. God made a covenant with Abraham, renewed it with Moses, confirmed it with David, proclaimed it through Isaiah and foretold its fulfilment in Jeremiah's prophecies. This covenant, which dealt not only with God's promise of land and prosperity for his people, was concerned, above all, with a personal relationship between God and his people. God would be their God, they would be his people. They would belong to God and the promise was not only for them but for their children.

This covenant of grace finally fulfilled in the New Testament, is describes by Paul like this:

> *"so that in Christ Jesus the blessing of Abraham might come to the Gentiles, so that we might receive the promised Spirit through faith"* (Galatians 3:14).

The really exciting thing about the covenant of grace is that it is personal. God's plan promises a personal relationship with himself and God accomplishes this plan through a personal Redeemer, Jesus Christ. Jesus God's Son redeems or releases us from the slavery of sin and brings us into a personal relationship with God. God's covenant is activated in us through God's Son our Redeemer.

On examination, God's plan through his Redeemer becomes even more intriguing, because who Christ is and what he did are vital to the outworking of the plan. This we must now investigate.

CHRIST

WHO HE IS

To learn about the person of Christ we must refer to the teaching of the Bible. Even a quick glance at the gospel accounts reveals that Jesus was more than a human. Indeed, those who have studied the subject in depth often describe Jesus as the God-man, meaning that Jesus had a divine as well as a human nature - that he had two natures united in one person. The early Church spent over three hundred years seeking an adequate definition of who Christ is, not simply because it was an important issue but because it was vital for God's plan of salvation.

DIVINE

The New Testament teaches that Jesus was fully God in at least three ways.

Works

Jesus often revealed that he was divine by his actions. He **healed** a whole variety of diseases in people who were blind, deaf and dumb, lame, paralysed and dying. In particular, with unfailing success, he dealt with extreme forms of illness such as leprosy, demon-possession, even raising the dead to life.

He performed **miracles**, thereby displaying absolute power in controlling and over-ruling the laws of nature. With five loaves and two fish he fed over five thousand people. He stilled a storm on the sea of Galilee.

His **teaching,** too, was unique. He taught with authority, but an authority far superior to the authority of the religious teachers of his day. Those sent to arrest him returned empty-handed, amazed at his power of speech.

Claims
Jesus' claims were stupendous. He asserted that he could **forgive sin**, that he was **all-powerful**, that he was one with God his Father.

> *"And when Jesus saw their faith, he said to the paralytic, 'Son, your sins are forgiven.'"* (Mark 2:5).

> *"And Jesus came and said to them, 'All authority in heaven and on earth has been given to me'"* (Matthew 28:18).

Confronting the Scribes and Pharisees, he expressed his superiority over Abraham and claimed **equality with God**, his words giving the impression that he was either a deluded madman or the Son of God.

> *"Jesus said to them, 'Truly, truly, I say to you, before Abraham was, I am'"* (John 8:58).

There is no middle position between these alternatives.

Reputation
The opinion of the apostles confirms Jesus' deity. To John he was the **eternal Word** who was God from the beginning.

> *"In the beginning was the Word, and the Word was with God, and the Word was God"* (John 1:1).

To Paul, he was in his **very nature, God** with no need to grasp at equality with God.

> *"who, though he was in the form of God, did not count equality with God a thing to be grasped"* (Philippians 2:6).

To the author of the letter to the Hebrews he was the **radiance of God's glory** and the exact representation of his being. Peter confesses that He is, *"the Son of the living God"* (Hebrews 1:3).

The Shorter Catechism sums it up like this.

> "The only Redeemer of God's elect is the Lord Jesus Christ, who, being the eternal Son of God became man, and so was and continues to be God and man, in two distinct natures and one person forever" (S.C. 21).

The deity of Christ is vital for our salvation. So disastrous were the results of sin in man's nature that mere sinful man, separated from God, could never accomplish anything before God on man's behalf. But, because of his divine nature, Christ, the Son of God, was able to redeem man from the slavery of sin. This is why he is, *"the **only** Redeemer of God's elect"* (S.C. 21). The initiative in solving the problem of man's sin had to come from God. It came in the divine person of the Son of God.

> *"All this is from God, who through Christ reconciled us to himself and gave us the ministry of reconciliation; that is, in Christ God was reconciling the world to himself, not counting their trespasses against them, and entrusting to us the message of reconciliation"* (II Corinthians 5:18, 19).

Cecil Frances Alexander puts it this way in her lovely hymn:

> "There was no other good enough
> To pay the price of sin;
> He only could unlock the gate
> Of heaven, and let us in".

HUMAN

We have seen from New Testament scripture that Christ was fully God. But the New Testament makes it clear that Christ is also human.

Life
The whole course of Christ's life is portrayed as human. We note this especially at the beginning of the gospel story. While his conception was supernatural, after the usual period of pregnancy, his birth was perfectly normal. Luke describes Jesus growing up in similar language to that which he uses for John the Baptist's childhood and youth (Luke 2:40, 52 cf. Luke 1:80).

Throughout the gospel story Jesus appears as a thoroughly human person. He experiences the full range of human emotions and sensations. He is **tired** and **thirsty** by the well at Sychar, **hungry** by the sea of Galilee, **tempted** by the devil in the desert, **angry** at the money-changers in the temple, **grieved** at the death of Lazarus and **frightened** in the garden of Gethsemane. While Christ never comes across as a "super-man" devoid of human feelings and emotions, he is obviously different.

> *"What sort of man is this, that even winds and sea obey him?"* (Matthew 8:27; John 4:6; Mark 11:12; Mark 11:15; John 11:35; Mark 14:34).

Impression
Christ's humanity is affirmed by the apostles in the clearest terms. **John** describes him as the word who became flesh, whom his friends handled, touched and looked at.

> *"But to all who did receive him, who believed in his name, he gave the right to become children of God"* (John 1:12).

The **writer to the Hebrews** claims that Christ did not take to himself an angelic nature but flesh and blood, the seed of Abraham.

> *"Since therefore the children share in flesh and blood, he himself likewise partook of the same things, that through death he might destroy the one*

> who has the power of death, that is, the devil"
> (Hebrews 2:14).

Paul notes that Christ was born of a woman, under the law, in the likeness of sinful flesh, yet without sin.

> "But when the fullness of time had come, God sent forth his Son, born of woman, born under the law" (Galatians 4:4).

All are convinced of Christ's humanity but in his case, a sinless humanity. The Shorter Catechism explains it in these terms:

> "Christ, the Son of God, became man by taking to himself a body and a soul like ours, being conceived by the power of the Holy Spirit in the womb of the Virgin Mary, and born of her, yet without sin" (S.C. 22).

Peter helps us understand the importance of Christ's humanity for salvation. He describes Christ as dying for sins once for all, the righteous for the unrighteous, "to bring you to God" using a word expressing the idea of one person bringing another into formal audience with a dignitary.

Christ, in his humanity, identifies with us in our weak human condition, sympathising with us and understanding our human lot. But he does more. As man, he comes down to our level, befriends us, forgives our sin and taking us by the hand, and reconciles us to God. How precious to us is his humanity.

WHAT HE DID

The study of what Christ did, is called the Work of Christ. The Shorter Catechism's summary is most helpful.

> "Christ as our Redeemer fills the offices of a prophet, of a priest and of a king, in his states both of humiliation and exaltation" (S.C. 23).

God's Plan

The *"state of humiliation and exaltation"* takes in the whole course of Christ's life; past, present and future. Christ's humiliation involves his birth itself, and that in lowly circumstances, his life facing constant opposition and his degrading death on the cross. His exaltation includes his resurrection from death, his ascension to God his Father, his position and privilege with God and his anticipated return as judge.

PROPHET

As a prophet, Christ proclaims God's Word to us – in particular how God planned to rescue us from sin.

> *"Christ fills the office of a prophet in revealing to us by his Word and Spirit the will of God for our complete salvation"* (S.C. 24).

Christ acts as a prophet by revealing God to us in his life. John the apostle, emphasises this theme. He reminds us that our only source of knowledge of God at this depth, comes through Christ alone.

> *"No one has ever seen God; the only God, who is at the Father's side, he has made him known"* (John 1:18).

Christ is God's exclusive Word to us, a theme which John develops later in his writings.

The other apostles comment on this prophetic work of Christ. The writer to the Hebrews describes Christ as God's final Word to mankind. God, who,

> *"Long ago, at many times and in many ways, God spoke to our fathers by the prophets, but in these last days he has spoken to us by his Son, whom he appointed the heir of all things, through whom also he created the world"* (Hebrews 1:1, 2).

Peter sees Christ as God's fulfilled Word to men.

> *"Concerning this salvation, the prophets who prophesied about the grace that was to be yours searched and inquired carefully, inquiring what person or time the Spirit of Christ in them was indicating when he predicted the sufferings of Christ and the subsequent glories.*
>
> *It was revealed to them that they were serving not themselves but you, in the things that have now been announced to you through those who preached the good news to you by the Holy Spirit sent from heaven, things into which angels long to look"* (I Peter 1:10, 11, 12).

The Spirit of Christ inspired the Old Testament prophets in their prophecies of a coming Messiah. Paul implies that Christ is God's full Word to us.

> *"For God, who said, 'Let light shine out of darkness," has shone in our hearts to give the light of the knowledge of the glory of God in the face of Jesus Christ'* (II Corinthians 4:6).

We discover his office as prophet in the earthly ministry of Jesus. Amid pressing concern to heal the sick, Jesus insists on moving on to other villages to preach there as well, for that was his purpose in coming to the world. He was a prophet over and above being a healer. The people were amazed at his teaching, *"a new teaching - and with authority"* was how they described it. It was obviously a superior teaching to that of the scribes and Pharisees. He spoke as a prophet with direct authority from God. Christ's teaching was aimed at instructing about salvation from sin through himself as Messiah. Praying for his disciples, Jesus says how he had given them God's Words, how his disciples had accepted this teaching and how, as a result, they had come to believe and know with certainty that he had been sent by God. Indeed, the very purpose governing the apostle John's selection of Jesus' teaching and deeds for his gospel account was that people might believe that,

God's Plan

> *"Jesus is the Christ, the Son of God, and that by believing they might have life in his name"* (John 20:31).

PRIEST

As a **priest**, Christ sacrificed his life for his people's sin and continually prays to God for them.

> *"But when Christ appeared as a high priest of the good things that have come, then through the greater and more perfect tent (not made with hands, that is, not of this creation) he entered once for all into the holy places, not by means of the blood of goats and calves but by means of his own blood, thus securing an eternal redemption. For if the blood of goats and bulls, and the sprinkling of defiled persons with the ashes of a heifer, sanctify for the purification of the flesh, how much more will the blood of Christ, who through the eternal Spirit offered himself without blemish to God, purify our conscience from dead works to serve the living God.*
>
> *Therefore he is the mediator of a new covenant, so that those who are called may receive the promised eternal inheritance, since a death has occurred that redeems them from the transgressions committed under the first covenant"* (Hebrews 9:11-15).

> "Christ fills the office of a priest in his once offering up of himself to God as a sacrifice, to satisfy divine justice and reconcile us to God; and in making constant intercession for us" (S.C. 25).

Stressing this aspect of Christ's work the writer to the Hebrews recalls how Christ's sacrifice was **personal** in that he offered not the blood of animals but his own blood. He maintains that Christ's sacrifice was **perfect** in as much as he offered himself *"unblemished"* to God, thereby providing not mere ceremonial purity but cleansing of conscience for his people. He affirms that Christ's sacrifice was **complete**. No other is needed. It was an unrepeatable act. Christ was sacrificed *"once for all"* to take away the sins of many people.

> "Not all the Blood of Beasts
> On Jewish, altars slain,
> Could give the guilty conscience peace
> Or wash away the stain:
> But Christ the heavenly Lamb
> Takes all our sins away
> A sacrifice of nobler name
> And richer Blood than they"
> (Isaac Watts)

Though this part of Christ's priestly work was completed there is another aspect of his priestly activity which continues. The writer to the Hebrews contrasts Christ our great high priest with the priests of Old Testament days. Jesus has a permanent priesthood because he lives forever: his sacrificial offering completed, he continues to intercede for his people. Christ is, therefore, able to save completely those who come to God through him.

> *"The former priests were many in number, because they were prevented by death from continuing in office, but he holds his priesthood permanently, because he continues forever. Consequently, he is able to save to the uttermost those who draw near to God through him, since he always lives to make intercession for them.*
>
> *For it was indeed fitting that we should have such a high priest, holy, innocent, unstained, separated from sinners, and exalted above the heavens. He has no need, like those high priests, to offer sacrifices daily, first for his own sins and then for those of the people, since he did this once for all when he offered up himself. For the law appoints men in their weakness as high priests, but the word of the oath, which came later than the law, appoints a Son who has been made perfect forever"* (Hebrews 7:23-28).

God's Plan

It is staggering to think on the one hand, of Christ's finished work, offered so long ago, providing complete cleansing from sin for his people and, on the other hand, to recall Christ's continuing intercession, pleading and praying to God his Father for his people day by day. Little wonder, then that the writer to the Hebrews describes Jesus as the mediator of a better covenant, a perfect priest who offered up a perfect sacrifice for his people.

KING

As a king, **Christ rules** over his people and defeats all their enemies.

> *"Christ fills the office of a king in making us his willing subjects, in ruling and defending us, and in restraining and conquering all his and our enemies"* (S.C. 26).

The gospel stories lead easily into the theme of Christ's kingship. This theme is evident at every point of Christ's earthly life.

Christ's birth was heralded by Isaiah as the birth of a child-Messiah who would rule over an eternal kingdom. The wise men sought information from Herod about one born king of the Jews. The angels told the shepherds about the birth of a Saviour, Christ the Lord in the royal city of David.

> *"For unto you is born this day in the city of David a Saviour, who is Christ the Lord"* (Luke 2:11).

> *"Now after Jesus was born in Bethlehem of Judea in the days of Herod the king, behold, wise men from the east came to Jerusalem, saying, 'Where is he who has been born king of the Jews? For we saw his star when it rose and have come to worship him.' When Herod the king heard this, he was troubled, and all Jerusalem with him; and assembling all the chief priests and scribes of the people, he inquired of them where the Christ was to be born. They told him, 'In*

> Bethlehem of Judea, for so it is written by the prophet:
>
> 'And you, O Bethlehem, in the land of Judah, are by no means least among the rulers of Judah; for from you shall come a ruler who will shepherd my people Israel'" (Matthew 2:1-6).

Christ's life also displayed his kingship. While he avoided popular aspirations to make him a political leader, Jesus nonetheless continued John the Baptist's message of an imminent kingdom. Throughout his teaching, Jesus made the demands of his rule clear, explaining these in the many parables of the kingdom which he told. Evidently, he saw his mission as establishing God's rule in men's lives and establishing that rule through unquestioning obedience to himself.

Even in his death the message of Christ's kingship comes to the fore. Jesus maintains before Pilate that he is a king, but a different kind of king from that in the mind of his accusers or from Pilate's perception of kingship. Jesus claims to rule over a kingdom of truth. That was the reason for his coming to this world. His followers do not fight, yet victory is certain. Pilate is sceptical but, perhaps, to a degree convinced, for he insists on the title over the cross remaining

> "Jesus of Nazareth, King of the Jews."

This is all part of God's plan of salvation, the covenant of grace, which God accomplishes through his Son the Redeemer. Christ, as Redeemer, is Mediator of God's covenant of grace. He brings God's plan of salvation to us.

Who Christ is, therefore, is vitally important. **He is the God-man, divine yet human**, high enough to gain God's ear on our behalf, low enough to take us by the hand and bring us to God. What Christ did is equally important. **As prophet**, he proclaims to man God's message of salvation. **As priest**, he died as a sacrifice to cleanse his people from sin and he constantly intercedes with God on their behalf. **As king**, he subdues rebellious man to himself, rules over him and defends him against all his enemies. God's plan provides everything for man's salvation. But it is a covenant of grace. It promises deliverance from sin only through Christ the Redeemer.

CONVERSION

God's plan of salvation is the "covenant of grace". It is a perfect plan, which can deal effectively with the sin problem in our lives. But how does the plan work and become personal? This is our next subject for study.

We might put the answer to the question like this. **God the Father plans salvation. God the Son provides salvation** but it is **God the Spirit** who **applies salvation** to our lives. He makes the plan work for us.

> *"We are made to share in the redemption purchased by Christ by the effective application of it to us by his Holy Spirit"* (S.C. 29).

God the Spirit does this through conversion. The word "conversion" is used in many different ways. We are using it to describe that complete change in life, where a person turns from sin to God, finds the answer to his sin problem in forgiveness and becomes a new person. Conversion is the door to salvation. Through conversion we become Christians, are born again into God's family and are saved from our sin. Conversion is the key to salvation.

GOD'S PART - REGENERATION

There are two parts to conversion. God's part and man's part. God has a part to play in a person becoming a Christian. But man is also involved.

God's part in salvation is called "regeneration". Regeneration means to "start over again", indeed "to be born again". In regeneration, God starts a person off on a new road of life. More than that. God makes a person into a new creation to start on that new road.

The Shorter Catechism uses the term "Effectual Calling" for regeneration. This is helpful. It says,

> *"Effectual calling is the work of God's Spirit, whereby, convincing us of our sin and misery, enlightening our minds in the knowledge of Christ, and renewing our wills, he doth persuade and enable us to embrace Jesus Christ, freely offered to us in the gospel"* (S.C. 31).

© "Confession of Faith and Subordinate Standards" The Free Church of Scotland

The Bible has a number of important things to say about regeneration.

SOVEREIGN

It teaches us that regeneration is a sovereign act, that is, God alone can regenerate. Man is powerless to do anything about that aspect of his conversion.

John the apostle stresses this. Introducing his gospel story, he uses the terms "children of God" and "born of God" to describe Christians. The terms are very significant. Physical birth was something which happened to us. So spiritual rebirth or regeneration is the same in principle. We do not cause it. It happens to us. This does not mean we are totally uninvolved in it, any more than we were totally uninvolved in our physical birth. John wants to make this perfectly clear. He writes,

> *"But to all who did receive him, who believed in his name, he gave the right to become children of God, who were born, not of blood nor of the will of the flesh nor of the will of man, but of God."* (John 1:12, 13).

NECESSARY

Jesus emphasised the necessity of regeneration. He told

God's Plan

Nicodemus, a renowned religious teacher, that he needed to be "born again". Without this rebirth, Jesus claimed, Nicodemus could neither see nor enter the kingdom of God. Indeed, Jesus goes even further in the way he expresses this truth. He insists that regeneration is absolutely necessary. Each and every one *"must be born again"* (John 3:7).

COMPLETE

Paul teaches that regeneration involves complete and total change. He puts it like this.

> *"Therefore, if anyone is in Christ, he is a new creation. The old has passed away; behold, the new has come"* (II Corinthians 5:17).

Something new comes into existence when a person is born again. An old life dies with its values and interests. A new life is born with fresh purpose. This new creation involves a total change, as radical as a change from death to life, from sin to God.

LIFE-GIVING WORD

There are two places, in the New Testament that teach what happens in regeneration. Though it is a sovereign work of God, it comes about through God's Word, the scriptures. Peter describes the Christians to whom he is writing as, *". . . you have been born again, . . . through the living and abiding word of God"* (I Peter 1:23) and later identifies that Word as having been preached to them. God had obviously used this gospel Word as imperishable seed among them. As they listened to the preaching of the gospel, God caused the seed to germinate and they were born again.

James describes regeneration like this.

> *"Of his (God) own will he brought us forth by the word of truth, that we should be a kind of first-fruits of his creatures"* (James 1:18).

The picture here is a vivid one. It is of God causing people to be born as a "new species" of his creation through his Word.

Some varieties of fish reproduce their young by spewing them out of their mouth. While an imperfect analogy, this picture helps illustrate the process of regeneration through the Word, of which James writes.

God's Spirit applies the benefits of the covenant of grace to our lives through regeneration. This is God's part in our conversion. Regeneration is a sovereign work. God alone causes it. It is a necessary work. We all need to be born again. It involves a complete change. One life ends, a new one begins. It is related to God's Word and so it involves us, our minds and wills. As we listen to the good news of salvation, God convinces us of our sin and misery, enlightens our minds in the knowledge of Christ and renewing our wills, persuades and enables us to embrace Jesus Christ freely offered to us in the gospel. God takes the initiative in regeneration. God the Spirit applies salvation to our lives.

MAN'S PART - REPENTANCE AND FAITH

Man has a vital part to play in conversion. In this, he responds to God's initiative of regeneration. Man's part in conversion has two aspects - repentance and faith. This is put very clearly when Paul was speaking to the Ephesian elders at Miletus. Paul was in a hurry but he took time to gather the elders together to speak to them. He reminded them how he had worked hard among them both physically and spiritually. He had worked with his own hands to be independent of them. He taught both publicly and from house to house. He sums up his work like this,

> "I did not shrink from declaring to you anything that was profitable, and teaching you in public and from house to house, testifying both to Jews and to Greeks of repentance toward God and of faith in our Lord Jesus Christ" (Acts 20:20, 21).

The task of bringing Jews and Greeks to God involves repentance and faith. Conversion, whatever our national or religious background, consists of these two ingredients -

God's Plan

repentance and faith.

REPENTANCE

The important thing about repentance, as the Bible describes it, is that it does not just mean feeling sorry for our sins. Of course, it includes that. Regret and remorse are always a part of repentance. But repentance in the New Testament means a "change of mind" and in the Old Testament, a "right-about turn". As well as feeling sorry about being a sinner, repentance means changing our minds, changing our direction in life, turning right around from sin and facing the opposite direction. Turning rather than feeling is the mark of true repentance.

The Shorter Catechism teaches

> *"Repentance leading to life is a saving grace by which a sinner having truly realised his sin and grasped the mercy of God in Christ, turns from his sin with grief and hatred and turns to God with full resolve and effort after new obedience"* (S.C. 87).

Complete

Repentance is an absolute turning from sin to God. Even the term the Shorter Catechism uses to describe repentance is significant. It is "Repentance unto life". If repentance meant only feeling sorry for sin and even turning from sin, it would be somewhat morbid, inward-looking and even hopeless. For there is little we ourselves can do about our sin but be sorry for it and try to stop sinning, and in this we inevitably fail.

Repentance, however, is more. It is "unto life". We turn from sin to God, and God solves the problem of our sin. So, while Ezekiel calls people to turn from judgment, John the Baptist urges them to turn in hope to God so that his kingdom may be established in their lives. Those "cut to the heart" by Peter's preaching repented because they were conscience-stricken. Paul, writing to the Corinthian Christians, maintains that,

"... Godly grief produces a repentance that leads to salvation without regret, whereas worldly grief produces death (II Corinthians 7:10).

True repentance is from judgment to hope, from sin to salvation. It is repentance "unto life".

Necessary
Jesus stresses the necessity of repentance. Some folk talking with Jesus had mentioned how Pilate had executed certain Galileans, mixing their blood with their sacrifices (Luke 13:1-5). Those speaking to Jesus seemed to imply that this had happened to these Galileans because they were sinful. Jesus sharply corrected their view, maintaining that, except they themselves would repent, they would all perish too. Jesus added that it was exactly the same with those eighteen, who died when the tower of Siloam fell on them. They were neither more nor less guilty than others living in Jerusalem. Jesus said, except his hearers all repented, they would all perish as well. From this, it seems clear that there are no exceptions. Regardless of the degree of our sinfulness, we are all sinners. Except we all repent, we will all perish. Each of us needs to repent.

FAITH

The second aspect in man's side of conversion is faith. Having turned around completely from sin to God man needs to have faith if he is to become a Christian. But what is faith? Faith means different things to different people. To some, it simply means a vague belief in the existence of God. To others, it is more definite than that. To such people faith means believing in God's power and goodness in such a way that, when there are troubles and difficulties in life, you can ask God to help and you really believe that he will help you. To many more, it is the belief that there is such a thing as the "supernatural" and that, behind life as we know it, there is a supernatural Power, who can intervene and change things. Some, then, see this kind of faith as

God's Plan

part of all religions. The common factors here are having a certain set of beliefs, vague or otherwise, and maintaining a personal degree of trust in these beliefs, strong or weak.

Those who have studied "faith" in the Bible tell us that there are three elements in it:
- "**knowledge**", we must know about the gospel;
- "**assent**", we must believe that it is true;
- "**trust**", we must trust the Saviour.

Notice how these three elements, **knowledge**, **assent** and **trust** include the two common factors we have already discovered, a set of beliefs and a personal degree of trust. The really important thing about the biblical teaching of faith is that it involves not just knowledge of certain facts, nor even mental assent to them but personal trust and, in the case of the gospel, this means personal trust in a personal Saviour. Head knowledge is not enough. The apostle James reminds us,

> *"You believe that God is one; you do well. Even the demons believe—and shudder!"* (James 2:19).

By no stretch of imagination could we regard demons as Christians.

Faith in biblical terms is personal trust in Jesus Christ as Saviour and Lord. The Shorter Catechism brings us to the very heart of the matter in its definition of faith,

> "Faith in Jesus Christ is a saving grace by which we receive and rest upon him alone for salvation as he is freely offered to us in the gospel" (S.C. 86).

That is the only kind of faith, which gets to the root of the matter and deals with the problem of our sin. In repentance we turn from our sin. In faith we receive Jesus Christ as both Saviour and Lord.

The Bible provides a number of very helpful pictures of this personal saving faith.

Come
Faith means coming to Christ with purpose. Jesus said,

> *"Come to me, all who labour and are heavy laden, and I will give you rest. Take my yoke upon you, and learn from me, for I am gentle and lowly in heart, and you will find rest for your souls. For my yoke is easy, and my burden is light"* (Matthew 11:28-30).

Obviously, Jesus was not just talking about being tired after a hard day's work. He was using that as an illustration of the frustration and weariness which sin produces in our lives. Rest for the soul and a purposeful new existence is found when we come to him to deal with our burden of sin and when we start serving him as master. Faith is coming to Christ with the purpose of getting rid of our sin and of finding a new life in him.

Receive
Faith involves receiving Christ with power. John stresses the difference it makes when we welcome Jesus as Messiah and Lord.

> *"But to all who did receive him, who believed in his name, he gave the right to become children of God"* (John 1:12).

Notice how John says that "receiving" Christ is the same thing as "believing in" Christ. We have faith in Christ, we believe in his name, by receiving him as Saviour. The glorious result is that we then have the right to regard ourselves as "born of God". To have faith in Christ means to receive him with power and this is invariably linked to our being born again. It is connected with our regeneration. Both sides of conversion, man's side and God's side are mentioned here.

Rely

Faith is relying on the person of Christ. This stresses the aspect of trust connected with faith. The Shorter Catechism emphasises this in its definition of faith,

> ". . . we receive and rest upon him alone for salvation . . ." (S.C. 86).

The New Testament underlines the personal involvement of this faith. The expression used for Jesus' words in John 3:16 conveys the sense of "believing into him". It is a complete personal involvement, like the child in the parent's arms. Protection, love and life are all provided. We *"shall not perish but have eternal life"*.

The New Testament also stresses the personal dependence involved in this faith. Paul's words to the distraught Philippian jailer could be rendered literally,

> *"Believe in the Lord Jesus, and you will be saved, you and your household"* (Acts 16:31).

In the jailer's distressing world, where nothing seemed secure, Paul preached Christ as a sure personal foundation, for both the jailer himself and his family.

Faith is relying on Christ intimately and completely to deliver us from sin and to give us new life.

Trust

Faith is trusting in the promises of Christ for salvation. It would be wrong to think of faith as personal trust in Christ, without regard for Christ's teaching. That would be like separating who Christ was from what Christ did. The purpose of Christ's life was to teach the good news of salvation from sin. Christ died to put that good news into effect. Personal faith in Christ inevitably involves trust in Christ's teaching about salvation and this must be an absolute, obedient trust.

In his gospel, John tells the story of Jesus healing a royal official's son. In the course of the story, Jesus urges the official to go home, for his son would live. John comments,

> *"The man believed the word that Jesus spoke to him and went on his way"* (John 4:50).

Later, when the official heard of his son's recovery, he inquired as to the precise time the boy started to get better. It was at the exact moment when Jesus had told him to go home that his son would live. As a result of this information, John observes about the official,

> *"And he himself believed, and all his household"* (John 4:53).

This story helps us to understand faith as trusting in the promises of Christ for salvation. The official simply took Jesus at his word. He did exactly what Jesus said. He obeyed, putting Jesus' words into practice. The result was as Jesus had claimed. On reflection, it drove the official and his family to a confirmed trust in Jesus. Faith in Jesus' word led to faith in Jesus' person for both the official and his family. As we obey Christ's teaching about salvation, we experience the result in our lives and it produces a personal trust in Christ.

God's Plan

SUMMARY

GOD'S PLAN

WHO CHRIST IS

Jesus Christ is human and divine.

1. Look up the following passages and write down under the appropriate heading what aspect of Jesus' humanity or divinity is being described.

John 11:35	Luke 8:22-25	Matthew 26:38
John 4:6	John 11:43-44	Mark 5:1-8
Luke 5:20-24	Luke 2:52	Mark 11:12

HUMAN CHARACTERISTICS	DIVINE CHARACTERISTICS

READ Hebrews 2:14-18

2. This passage speaks of Jesus and suggests some of the ways in which we may benefit from his humanity. Find out what these benefits are and write them down.

_____

_____

_____

_____

What Presbyterians Believe

WHAT CHRIST DID

The Shorter Catechism describes the work of Christ in terms of prophet, priest and king.

CHRIST AS PROPHET

1. Look up Deuteronomy 18:18. In this verse God is speaking through Moses. From this verse, describe what a prophet is.

   _____

A prophet is one who declares the words of God. Now look up John 1:14. Notice how Jesus Christ not only speaks the word of God, but he is "The Word".

CHRIST AS PRIEST

2. From Hebrews 5:1 describe in your own words the role of the Jewish High Priest.

   _____
   _____
   _____
   _____

3. Look up Hebrews 7:23-25 and Hebrews 10:11-12. How does Christ's sacrifice differ from what is offered by the Jewish priests?

   N.B. "this priest" (10:12) refers to Christ.

JEWISH PRIESTS	CHRIST'S PRIESTHOOD

God's Plan

CHRIST AS KING

4. Old Testament prophecy emphasises that the Kingdom established through David will last for ever. The Messiah therefore, is anticipated in terms that suggests kingship. Look up Isaiah 9:6-7 and describe the features of Messianic kingship.

_____

_____

_____

_____

_____

_____

5. Now look at these references from the Gospels and set out the evidence for recognising Jesus as the great Messiah-King.

    Matthew 1:1   Matthew 2:2   Luke 19:37-38
    John 18:33-37   Matthew 28:18

_____

_____

_____

_____

_____

_____

_____

_____

What Presbyterians Believe

CONVERSION

GOD'S SIDE

Regeneration - this term means "rebirth".

1. Look up the following references which contain phrases linked to the doctrine of regeneration. Write out the appropriate words.

   John 1:12-13 _____

   I Peter 1:23 _____

   2 Corinthians 5:17 _____

Note how in all these statements the initiative comes from God.

Now look up John 3:8.

2. This verse comes in the middle of Jesus' conversation with Nicodemus. What illustration does Jesus use to describe the regenerating work of the Holy Spirit?

   _____
   _____
   _____

3. You cannot see the wind, but you can observe the effects of it, e.g. fallen tree branches. Similarly, you cannot see the Spirit, but, like the wind, the effect of it can be observed. Can you add to the example given here? e.g. turning away from sinful things.

   _____
   _____

MAN'S SIDE

4. What are the twin elements in man's response to God?

   _____
   _____

50

God's Plan

5. What does repentance mean?

   _____

   _____

6. What are the essential elements of faith contained in the text?

   _____

   _____

Read Luke 19:1-10

7. Can you pick out from this story of Zacchaeus's conversion some of the elements of repentance and faith? List them below.

   _____

   _____

   _____

   _____

CHAPTER 4

NEW LIFE

THE NEW YOU

God is holy, man is sinful. God provides the remedy for man's sin in the covenant of grace. God's plan of salvation. It is a perfect plan because the mediator of the covenant is Jesus Christ, the Redeemer, the God-man. It is also a personal plan. God regenerates sinful man to see in Jesus Christ the answer to his sin. In conversion, through repentance and faith. God enables sinful man to receive Jesus Christ as Saviour and man is saved from his sin. People often think, however, because God has done so much for us in salvation that there is nothing for us to do. We simply wait until God does something to us. If we are to be "converted", we imagine that we must feel right about it. So, many are waiting for some great emotional upheaval before they respond to the gospel. They think that the only true way to come to faith in Christ is at an appeal given at the close of a service or mission meeting. Only when they "feel" right will they come.

Conversion is not like that. God has provided a perfect plan and takes the initiative in regeneration but we must respond. That is our responsibility. The Bible makes it clear that it is an urgent responsibility in which we must make the effort. Jesus tells people to seek his kingdom as a priority. He says that we should strive to enter it. Paul claims that God now commands all men everywhere to repent. It is an urgent, universal summons, in which our minds and wills are far more important than our feelings.

We should not be put off by worries about how we ought to "feel" in conversion. Conversion is a decisive but not necessarily a dramatic emotional experience. Conversion is not gradual in the sense that one day we wake up and find ourselves converted. We must seek, strive and enter the door of conversion. **Paul's** conversion was **dramatic**. **Lydia's** was **quiet** and **gentle**. God opened Lydia's heart to respond to Paul's instruction. It is a personal matter between you and God.

Whenever we become Christians, certain things happen to us. The Bible gives some helpful pictures of these things. It is important for us to study them.

JUSTIFICATION

When we become Christians we receive justification. The Shorter Catechism defines justification,

> *"Justification is an act of God's free grace in which he pardons all our sins and accepts us as righteous in his sight for the sake of the righteousness of Christ alone, which is credited to us and received by faith alone"* (S.C. 33).

Justification is the action of God as judge acquitting us of our sin because of Christ's righteousness.

Justification affects our standing before God. The scene is that of the law court. God is judge. We are the criminals condemned before God because of our sin. Justification resolves the situation. Paul has this picture in his mind as he explains justification to the Christians at Rome. All mankind, heathen, Greek and Jew are guilty before God. There is no-one righteous. God sends Christ through whom guilty man is justified or acquitted before God the judge.

> *"for all have sinned and fall short of the glory of God, and are justified by his grace as a gift, through the redemption that is in Christ Jesus"* (Romans 3:23, 24).

God justifies the sinner by reckoning Christ's righteousness to him. It is as though we had a dreadful overdraft in the bank, which we had no hope of paying, and someone deposited a vast sum to our account. Our standing is immediately changed. We are no longer debtors but creditors. Credit has been "reckoned" or "imputed" to us. In justification, Christ paid the debt of our sin. David speaks of the blessedness of the man to whom God

New Life

credits righteousness apart from works:

> *"Blessed are those whose lawless deeds are forgiven, and whose sins are covered: blessed is the man against whom the Lord will not count his sin"* (Romans 4:6,7, 8) cf. Psalm 32.

Being justified, our sense of guilt disappears. While we remain truly sorry for the sin in our lives, we are no longer condemned for it. No-one can condemn us for God has justified us. We gain this standing through nothing in ourselves but totally through faith in Jesus Christ.

> *"Jesus thy blood and righteousness*
> *My beauty are, my glorious dress*
> *'Midst flaming worlds in these arrayed*
> *With joy shall lift up my head.*
> *Bold shall I stand in that great day*
> *For who ought to my charge shall lay?*
> *Fully absolv'd through Thee I am*
> *From sin and fear, from guilt and shame."*
> (Nikolaus L. von Zinzendorf)

ADOPTION

When we become Christians we are adopted into God's family.

> *Adoption is an act of God's free grace by which we are received into the number and have a right to all the privileges of the sons of God"* (S.C. 34).

Adoption affects our relationship with God. Adopting a child is a wonderful, kind and good action. A married couple of their own freewill give a baby a home and a family. As the baby grows up, he calls his adoptive parents "mummy" and "daddy", something he may well not have been able to do had he not been adopted. He shares in family life, its joys and sorrows, its companionship and purpose, its security and comfort. In all probability, when his adoptive parents die, he inherits their possessions for he "belongs" to them and so what is theirs "belongs" to him. The relationship of adoption has shaped the entire life of this chosen child.

The New Testament teaches that, in salvation, we are adopted by God. Paul stresses the privileges of this adoption. All Christians are God's children through faith in Jesus Christ. They address God intimately in prayer calling, Abba, Father. As heirs of God and co-heirs with Christ, they share a life not only of suffering but ultimately of glory. They live together as brothers and sisters with other Christians in the family of God and under God's loving fatherhood.

John emphasises the wonder of this adoption. Christians have the right to regard themselves as children of God. This shows God's great love for them. Family likeness becomes theirs by adoption. They look forward eventually to being like Christ in holiness.

SANCTIFICATION

When we become Christians, sanctification begins in our lives. But what is sanctification? Sanctification is holiness or godliness, the absence of sin and evil, the presence of goodness and righteousness, in the life of the Christian. The Shorter Catechism defines sanctification as,

> *"Sanctification is the work of God's free grace by which we are renewed throughout in the image of God and are enabled more and more to die to sin and live to righteousness"* (S.C. 35).

Sanctification affects our living for God. Notice the distinction the Shorter Catechism makes in defining justification and sanctification. Justification is described as an **"act"**, sanctification as a **"work"**. Justification is **instantaneous**, sanctification is **continuous**. God alone justifies. Both God and man are active in sanctification.

This means that sanctification is a growth process, in which the Christian is actively involved. The New Testament bears this out. While Paul insists that salvation is not of works but by faith, he describes Christians as God's workmanship created in Jesus

New Life

Christ for good works. They are to "work out" the salvation which God has "worked into" them. The evidence of this will be in the "fruit" of the Spirit in their lives, the growth produced by God working in them. Peter maintains that Christians are to make their calling and election sure by adding to their faith a number of features indicating personal godliness. If so, they will be fruitful and effective. If not, they will be short-sighted and blind, forgetting the past sins from which they have been cleansed. James tells us that faith without works is dead.

There are two vivid pictures in the New Testament of sanctification. One is a change of clothing. We take off the old nature of sin. We put on the new nature of godliness. Paul develops this theme writing to the Ephesians. They must take off darkness, lying and anger. They must put on light, truth and love. In this way, they will be putting off the old self, which is being corrupted by its deceitful desires. They will be putting on the new self, created to be like God in true righteousness and holiness. It is a continuous process and involves effort.

The other picture of sanctification is that of the Christian dying with Christ in his death and coming alive with Christ in his resurrection. We are dead with Christ to sin, we come alive with Christ to righteousness. Paul writes,

> *"We were buried therefore with him by baptism into death, in order that, just as Christ was raised from the dead by the glory of the Father, we too might walk in newness of life"* (Romans 6:4).

This is a remarkable encouragement to righteousness for the Christian.

There is a difference of opinion concerning the application of sanctification in a Christian's life. Some suggest that at conversion we come to Christ as Saviour but, at a later point, we receive the "baptism of the Spirit", surrender to Christ as Lord and obtain sanctification. This is regarded as a second work of grace and is commonly called "a second blessing". However, Presbyterians maintain that at conversion we come to Christ as

Saviour and Lord, experience the "baptism of the Spirit", and then continue to grow in a process of holiness. At conversion, we are justified. Thereafter, we begin a life process of sanctification or growth in holy living.

ASSURANCE

The result of justification, adoption and sanctification, which we receive when we become Christians, is assurance of salvation. These things make us sure that we have truly become Christians, that our conversion is real, not counterfeit, that we are born again as children of God with a new nature and that we will continue to grow and develop as Christians. They encourage our weak faith to be strong as we start out on the Christian life. The Shorter Catechism lists these benefits in detail.

> *"The benefits in this life which accompany or flow from justification, adoption and sanctification are: assurance of God's love, peace of conscience, joy in the Holy Spirit, progress in holiness, and perseverance in it to this life's end"* (S.C. 36).

When people take the step of faith in Christ, they often have many doubts and fears. Frequently, they rely on their feelings and, as their feelings are either high or low, so they judge as to whether they really have become Christians or not. The Bible teaches us not to rely primarily on feelings but on God's promises for assurance of salvation. When we recall the promises of God to which we responded as we took the step of faith, it brings peace to our hearts. These promises remind us that as we came to Christ, God acquitted us of our sins, adopted us as his children and started us off as new persons on a new life of holiness. **We are justified by faith and so have peace with God.** God's Spirit comes alongside our conscience and tells us that we are God's children. God has begun a work in us and will complete it

> *". . . being confident of this, that he who began a good work in you will carry it on to completion until the day of Christ Jesus"* (Philemon 1:6). (NIV)

Recalling God's promises enables us to deal effectively with

New Life

our feelings of doubt.

Seeing the fulfilment of those promises encourages our spiritual growth. As we watch our interests change and come to love God's Word, prayer and meeting with other Christians in worship and instruction, it confirms our faith. As we find the fruit of the Spirit developing in our lives and changing our character at home and at work, it makes us sure that God is at work in us and that we have truly become Christians.

> *"But the fruit of the Spirit is love, joy, peace, patience, kindness, goodness, faithfulness, gentleness, self-control . . ."* (Galatians 5:22f).

THE FRIENDS OF THE NEW LIFE

Justification, adoption and sanctification bring assurance to the Christian. They are "means" or instruments of grace to him. They are his new-found friends in the Christian life. They are "inner" friends, for God works through these means "within" the Christian, assuring him that he is now a child of God.

The Christian has also "outer" friends. The Shorter Catechism calls these "the outward and ordinary means". God provides certain help "outside" the Christian to assist him in his growth in grace.

> *"The outward and ordinary means whereby Christ communicateth to us the benefits of redemption, are his ordinances, especially the Word, sacraments, and prayer; all which are made effectual to the elect for salvation"* (S.C. 88).
> © *"Confession of Faith and Subordinate Standards" The Free Church of Scotland*

There is an excellent summary of these **"outward, and ordinary means"** in Acts 2:42.

> *"And they devoted themselves to the apostles' teaching and the fellowship, to the breaking of bread and the prayers"* (Acts 2:42).

There are four means mentioned here as absorbing the early Church's interest and attention:

- **Instruction**,
- **Fellowship** or sharing with one another,
- **Breaking of bread** (which may refer to the remembrance meal which we call the Lord's Supper),
- **Prayer**

As we will be studying the sacraments of Baptism and the Lord's Supper later, we will now examine the other **"outward means"** the Word of God, prayer and fellowship.

WORD OF GOD

The Shorter Catechism reminds us that

> *"The Word of God, which, consists of the scriptures of the Old and New Testaments, is the only rule to direct us how to glorify and enjoy him"* (S.C. 2).

As we consider the teaching of Christ and the apostles in the New Testament and think of how highly they viewed the Old Testament, we can well understand why the early Church devoted themselves to the apostles' teaching. It was also God's Word and they needed its instruction to inform their minds and direct their lives. God has given us the outward means of the Bible as the Word of God to help us in our Christian lives. We follow its instruction because it is God's Word. Scripture itself claims to be "God-breathed" and to have come into existence under the direction of God's Spirit. God is the author of the Bible. He has brought it into being. He speaks to us through it. **For that reason alone, it should be an absorbing interest for every Christian.**

The Bible is a help in two directions in particular. It helps toward conversion and it assists Christian growth.

> *"The Spirit of God maketh the reading, but especially the preaching of the Word, an effectual means of convincing and converting sinners, and of building them up in holiness and comfort, through faith, unto salvation"* (S.C. 89).

© "Confession of Faith and Subordinate Standards" The Free Church of Scotland

New Life

It was because scripture informed, taught, enlightened and ultimately convinced Timothy about salvation through faith in Christ that he is to continue studying it.

> *"But as for you, continue in what you have learned and have firmly believed, knowing from whom you learned it and how from childhood you have been acquainted with the sacred writings, which are able to make you wise for salvation through faith in Christ Jesus"* (II Timothy 3:14, 15).

As it was the "**means**" which led him to faith, so it should be his continuing delight in faith. When we consider how God used the preaching of the Word to enlighten us and to convince us of our need to come to Christ, it should be our natural interest now that we are Christians. Paul also reminds Timothy of the importance of scripture for developing the Christian life.

> *"All Scripture is breathed out by God and profitable for teaching, for reproof, for correction, and for training in righteousness, that the man of God may be competent, equipped for every good work"* (II Timothy 3:16, 17).

When we study the Bible we find instruction which directs us, warnings which correct us, promises which inspire us and practical advice which trains us. The Bible is God's perfect instruction manual. It equips the Christian for every kind of holy living and service.

Our attitude to the Bible should be urgent and intense. The Shorter Catechism reminds us,

> *"That the Word may become effectual to salvation, we must attend thereunto with diligence, preparation, and prayer; receive it with faith and love, lay it up in our hearts, and practice it in our lives"* (S.C. 90).

© "Confession of Faith and Subordinate Standards" The Free Church of Scotland

This means that we will desire to know God's Word, seeking its instruction like an infant craving for milk or an adult for food. We will think deeply about its truths, hiding its principles in our hearts, mixing our hearing with faith in case we lose its benefit. We will practice its teaching with determination, applying it practically and rigorously to our lives each day.

We will study the Bible at home privately but it is essential that we pay particular attention to the preaching of God's Word at church and mid-week meeting. God's Word will be a priority in our Christian lives. We will be devoted to it since God speaks to us through it and thereby equips us totally for Christian living.

PRAYER

Another friend of the new life is prayer. What is prayer? For many people prayer is no more than asking God for things. This is one aspect of prayer. David prayed for victory over his enemies. Hezekiah requested God to prolong his life. Elijah prayed for rain. Jesus taught us to ask, seek and knock in prayer. We must keep on praying until we get an answer. Paul described prayer as "supplications and intercessions". This means praying to God for both things and people. Christians undoubtedly find much help in asking God for things and in receiving them. Prayer is a help in that basic way but prayer benefits Christians in a much deeper way.

Prayer helps develop the Christian's personal relationship with God. The Catechism for young children describes prayer as,

> *"asking God for things* **which he has promised to give"** (Q.105).

Prayer is not just asking God for anything. **Prayer is asking God for things that agree with his will.** The Shorter Catechism gives a fuller description of prayer along the same lines.

> *"Prayer is an offering up of our desires to God, for things agreeable to his will, in the name of Christ, with confession of our sins and thankful acknowledgement of his mercies"* (S.C. 98).

New Life

Jesus' life and teaching confirm this. Jesus insists that we should ask God for things in his name, which means asking not only on Christ's authority but according to his will. In Gethsemane, Jesus resigned himself to God's will. He prayed that God's glory would be obvious in his death, for that had been his desire throughout life. Jesus encourages us to come to God as a father, who knows what we need before we ask and who will only give us what will be good for us. Jesus sees prayer as asking God for things which **he has promised to give.**

When Christians pray like this, it develops their personal relationship with God. They are talking to their heavenly Father. They are asking primarily not for what they want but for what God wants. They are distinguishing between their needs and their desires. They are conditioning their longings to what God has promised. They are talking and listening not just asking. This also helps with the problem of unanswered prayer. God's answer is sometimes "no" not "yes". When it is "no", Christians realise that they are seeking something God has not promised, at least, not for the present.

Prayer also helps the Christian by bringing about God's will. The God who has appointed the end has also appointed the means to that end and through prayer he gives us the privilege of asking and then of seeing his will performed. This is why the Shorter Catechism spends so much time explaining how we should pray. (S.C. 99-107)

> *"The whole word of God is of use to direct us in prayer, but the Special rule of direction is that form of prayer which Christ taught his disciples, commonly called The Lord's Prayer"* (S.C. 99).

Prayer is conversation with God. God directs the conversation and we respond. For this reason, it is much more helpful to read the Bible before we pray. We listen to God speaking first, then we respond in prayer. We must not change the subject or commandeer the conversation. Our prayer life often becomes dull and formal because it is "one-sided". As we use the whole Word of God to direct our praying, it will rescue us from this pit-fall.

The pattern of the Lord's Prayer emphasises the importance of God's will in prayer. It is addressed to a Creator who is our Father, whose character is perfect, whose sovereignty is universal, whose will is supreme, whose glory is absolute. We pray for God's glory. For ourselves, we seek God's care and forgiveness. Submission to God's will is the pattern of true prayer. Prayer is a means of bringing about God's will in our lives. Prayer marked the lives of all the great Old Testament characters. Jesus, in his teaching, constantly encouraged prayer showing it to be the only means through which man could do great works for God. Jesus' own practice of prayer is the greatest challenge to every Christian about his need for prayer. The apostles repeatedly stress the importance of prayer for the Christian life. We must pray without ceasing. The fervent prayer of the righteous man is powerful and effective.

Prayer is not just a help for the Christian but a necessity. Prayer develops our relationship with God and involves us in the accomplishment of God's will. Regular prayer at home and attendance at corporate prayer at church and prayer meetings are a first priority for the Christian. Prayer is the Christian's vital breath. By prayer he lives the Christian life. Prayer is absolutely essential for his well-being and growth in grace.

FELLOWSHIP

Fellowship is more than friendship. Secular clubs and groups enjoy friendship. Christians experience fellowship. Fellowship is literally "sharing", "holding something together in common". Christians are bonded together by their faith in Christ. They share Christ together. They have a common salvation. Fellowship was another of the outer means to which the first Christians devoted themselves.

Fellowship helps confirm Christians in their faith. This means making public our step of faith. Paul reminds the Roman Christians that we believe with the heart and are justified and confess with the mouth and are saved. He recalls Timothy to the good confession he had made before many witnesses. We must take our stand openly about becoming a Christian. We must not be ashamed of Christ before men. Secret discipleship weakens our position. Public confession strengthens faith. Continuing in fellowship with other Christians develops this process. It provides both instruction and correction. The New Testament urges Christians to mutual encouragement, restoration, submission, confession of sin, prayer and practical help. We must be willing to receive instruction and correction from each other. We can be encouraged together as we study God's Word and sing about God's greatness and goodness in praise.

Fellowship helps establish and extend the church. The fellowship of the early church was intensely practical. The first Christians shared possessions and sold land for the common good. The pattern continued as the church grew. They cared for widows, gossiped the gospel, gathered money for the cause, accepted advice from other Christians, commissioned missionaries and prayed for the work.

The church eventually straddled the Middle East and the Mediterranean in differing centres of varying nationalities. Yet there was a bond of unity. They were brothers and sisters in Christ, members of Christ's body, the church. As they shared their faith and their possessions, these Christians were established as a group and extended. Fellowship was a vital ingredient in their togetherness and their growth as a church.

The friends of the new life are "inner" and "outer". Justification, adoption and sanctification produce assurance within the Christian. The outer friends are equally important. The Word of God, which helped bring him to faith, also assists his growth as a Christian. Prayer develops his relationship with God and the realisation of God's will in his life. Fellowship with other Christians confirms and establishes his faith and extends it to others. The Word of God, prayer, fellowship and the sacraments then, are priorities. They are the Christian's best friends in the new life.

Some of these friends or "means" the Christian enjoys privately at home. Some he enjoys with others in the church. We must now study what the church means, as this is a very important part of the Christian's life.

New Life

SUMMARY

NEW LIFE

THE NEW YOU

1. Look up the following verses and write down what is new about the Christian.

   Romans 6:4   New _____
   II Corinthians 5:17 New _____
   Ephesians 4:24   New _____
   I Peter 1:3   New _____

JUSTIFICATION

2. Look up Romans 3:23 and say why we need to be justified.

   _____
   _____

3. From Romans 3:28, how are we justified?

   _____
   _____

   Complete the sentence by referring to Romans 4:25.

   We are not justified by "faith in my faith", but faith in

   _____

Compare Shorter Catechism Question 33.

ADOPTION

5. Does every human being have the right to call himself a child of God? If not, who is entitled to this privilege? See John 1:10-13.

_____
_____
_____
_____
_____

6. Study Galatians 4:4-7 and list some of the privileges of being adopted into God's family.

_____
_____
_____
_____

See Shorter Catechism Question 34.

SANCTIFICATION

7. Study Colossians 3:8-14. The following words are mixed up. Sort them out and list them under the appropriate headings.

Kindness	rage	compassion
Slander	greed	love
Patience	gentleness	filthy language
forgiving one another		sexual immorality

New Life

Things to put off	Things to put on

See Shorter Catechism question 35.

ASSURANCE

8. The phrase "we know" occurs frequently in the first letter of John. Look up the following references and list the evidence that help us to be assured of our salvation.

I John 2:3 - "We know" because _____

I John 3:14 - "We know" because _____

I John 5:18 - "We know" because _____

THE FRIENDS OF THE NEW LIFE

WORD OF GOD

9. The following references tell us that the Bible is like certain well known objects. Look up each reference and write down one sentence saying in what way the Bible is like this object. The first one is done for you as an example.

James 1:23-24
The Bible is like a *mirror* because *it shows me myself as I really am.*
Psalm 119:105
The Bible is like a _____ because _____

I Peter 2:2
The Bible is like _____ because _____

Ephesians 6:17
The Bible is like a _____ because _____

PRAYER

10. The Lord's Prayer, or disciples' prayer as it probably should be called, is like a model prayer for each Christian. It can be and often is repeated word for word, but each phrase suggests a subject that should be our concern in prayer. Study the prayer in Matthew 6:9-13 phrase by phrase under two headings - God and Me. The first one in each heading is done for you.

GOD	ME
Verse 9	Verse 11
Our Heavenly Father	Daily Bread or my needs for each day.
Verse 10 a	Verse 12
Verse 10 b	Verse 13

FELLOWSHIP

11. In the N.I.V. translation of Acts 2:42-47 the section is headed "The Fellowship of the Believers." Study this passage and list everything they did within their fellowship.

_____   _____

_____   _____

_____   _____

_____   _____

_____   _____

CHAPTER 5

CHURCH

The Scriptures teach us that our new-found faith, though personal, brings us into a new relationship with others as members of the church. While God calls individuals to himself, his purpose is to form,

> *"a chosen people, a royal priesthood, a holy nation,
> a people belonging to God"* (I Peter 2:9). (NIV)

While God's ultimate purpose is a perfect church (Ephesians 5:26f), here on earth the church is a means to that end as God's people meet together to worship, study, pray and enjoy fellowship together.

THE CHURCH AND HER HEAD

When people hear the word "church" they often think of a building. However, in the Bible "church" means people. God's people, rather than a building.

In both Old and New Testaments the words used for "church" literally mean those who are "called out" and "called together". The basic idea is of a people called out from a sinful world and called together to meet with God. Hence whenever these people meet to worship God, we speak of them as "going to church".

What a great help church is for the Christian. 'Going to church' means meeting with other Christians, listening to God speak through his Word, talking to God in prayer, singing about God's greatness in praise and sharing interest in God with other Christians

> *"And let us consider how we may spur one another
> on towards love and good deeds. Let us not give up
> meeting together, as some are in the habit of doing,
> but let us encourage one another – and all the more
> as you see the Day approaching"*
> (Hebrews 10:24-25). (NIV)

Church, then, for the Christian is a further means of grace, another outward help in developing his relationship with God. The Christian gets to know God better not only at home but also at church. Sometimes it can be lonely as a Christian whereas, at church with other Christians, our faith is brightened and developed. That was the reason why the first Christians, who were added to the church, *". . . devoted themselves to the apostles' teaching and to the fellowship, to the breaking of bread and to prayer"* (Acts 2:42).

For that reason, they continued to meet together every day in the temple courts,

> *"And day by day, attending the temple together and breaking bread in their homes, they received their food with glad and generous hearts, praising God and having favor with all the people."* (Acts 2:46, 47).

Church helps Christians develop their relationship with God and with each other. In the New Testament there are some vivid descriptions of the Church that helps us to understand how best we can use church to promote personal growth in grace and fellowship with other Christians.

VINE

Jesus teaches that he is the true or genuine vine, that God, his Father, is the gardener and that his disciples are branches (John 15:1-8). This is a meaningful description, since Israel, God's people, was, in the Old Testament, seen as a vine. The picture of the vine has a lot to say about the life Christians enjoy in their relationship with God and with other Christians. It reminds us that we have that life only as we are linked by saving faith to Christ, just as the branch only has life as it is joined to the trunk of the tree. It teaches that our purpose as Christians is to grow and to produce the fruit of godly living.

> *"But the fruit of the spirit is love, joy, peace, patience, kindness, goodness, faithfulness, gentleness, self-control . . ."* (Galatians 5:22, 23).

God the gardener prunes our lives to make us more fruitful. Bearing fruit is our reason for existence. Dead withered branches are useless. They are thrown away. These truths would instruct us to be fruitful by remaining in Christ through the Word and prayer.

> *"If you abide in me, and my words abide in you, ask whatever you wish, and it will be done for you. By this my Father is glorified, that you bear much fruit and so prove to be my disciples"* (John 15:7, 8).

In addition, the idea of the vine shows that, as branches, we have this life in common with all other Christians, for we are all linked by faith to Christ. The church is "one". Joined to Christ we share in one salvation, a oneness or unity seen in the Bible as a characteristic of the church. We need to remember that "togetherness" characterises Christians and that in our togetherness as a church we grow and bear fruit. Together, as well as individually, we study God's Word and pray.

BODY

Paul teaches that the church is the body of Christ. This reminds Christians how active they ought to be in their relationship with Christ and with one another. Paul uses two interesting pictures of the body to develop this idea of activity.

Writing to the churches at Rome and Corinth, Paul stresses that Christians are parts or members of the body of Christ. Basically, he is saying that they are all one, that they are all part of Christ's one body. But he expands this theme, suggesting that just as we have many limbs and organs in our human bodies, which do not all have the same function, so it is with the church, Christ's body. There are many different people making up the church but all are one, being linked by faith to Christ in his body. Yet, just as eyes and ears, the hands and feet have different functions within the human body, each with a different part to play, are all equally necessary.

This is important. It means that each Christian is needed

within the church. One Christian ought not to look down on another because his part seems insignificant. We are all equally important and necessary, but within the church, our function varies. We should, therefore, respect one another, recognising our differing functions, developing our individual part and encourage others to do the same.

Writing to the Christians at Colosse and Ephesus, Paul deploys his second picture of the church as the body of Christ. Here, he teaches that the church is the body of which Christ is the head. And just as the brain in a person's head controls and directs the body, so Christ, the head, controls and directs the church.

Paul also mentions a growing process here. He sees Christians growing up under Christ's Lordship into Christ the head of the body. He speaks of joints and ligaments all co-operating in growth and activity. This picture emphasises progress as well as variety of activity in the church. As Christians, each developing his particular gift, we should be growing and maturing in the Christian life within the church. Church activity should not wear us out but rather stimulate our service and develop our growth. The idea of the church as "catholic" or "universal", while implying the inclusion of all nations and of all ages in the church, is also evident in the picture of the body. Varied in function and progressive in growth, Christians in the church come from every race and area – and yet are one in Christ.

BRIDE

Paul depicts the church as the bride of Christ. This emphasises the love involved in the relationship between the church and Christ. Paul is writing practical words of advice to Christian husbands and wives in his letter to the Ephesians and uses the picture of the church as the bride of Christ to teach some important truths. This picture of the church is warm, affectionate and full of feeling. Christian wives are to submit to their husbands just as the church submits to Christ as Lord. Christian husbands are to love their wives just as Christ loves the church.

Church

That love must be a sacrificial love, since Christ gave himself for the church, and a purposeful love because Christ died both to cleanse the church from sin through the Word and to make the church holy, *"without stain or wrinkle or other blemish"* (Ephesians 5:27).

And it must be a caring love, since Christ feeds and cares for the church. As the church loves Christ, she grows in holiness. Yet while it is a warm love and full of feeling, it is neither sentimental nor sloppy. It is marked by obedience and self-sacrifice. It is full of purpose and practical caring. It is the kind of love of which Jesus spoke. It does good even to enemies and is not concerned overmuch about feelings. Such love has a purifying effect, producing holiness. Holiness, therefore, is one of the leading marks of the church. The church is "holy".

TEMPLE

Peter describes the church as the temple or house of God.

> *"As you come to him, a living stone rejected by men but in the sight of God chosen and precious, you yourselves like living stones are being built up as a spiritual house, to be a holy priesthood, to offer spiritual sacrifices acceptable to God through Jesus Christ. For it stands in Scripture:*
>
> *'Behold, I am laying in Zion a stone, a cornerstone chosen and precious, and whoever believes in him will not be put to shame.'*
>
> *So the honour is for you who believe, but for those who do not believe,*
>
> *'The stone that the builders rejected has become the cornerstone,' and*
> *'A stone of stumbling, and a rock of offense.'*
>
> *They stumble because they disobey the word, as they were destined to do"* (I Peter 2:4-8).

Peter sees Christians as those who have come to Christ and, as stones suddenly become alive. They are *"living stones"* (I Peter

2:4, 5) and are built into a "spiritual house" or living temple, in which sacrifices acceptable to God through Jesus Christ are offered. This idea of the church as the temple or house of God stresses the importance of service in our relationship to God and to other Christians. We are saved to serve. Serving God should be the natural and inevitable outcome of being living stones in the living temple of God. The New Testament speaks of praise, good works, sharing with others and a holy active life dedicated to God as "spiritual sacrifices" which Christians ought to be offering. Christ's life within us should move us to active service of this kind.

Service for the Christian is based on his relationship with Christ. Peter here describes Christ as the *"cornerstone"* (I Peter 2:4-8). The cornerstone dictates the shape of the building. It gives the building line and appearance. Christ the cornerstone directs Christians, as a church. He orders the form, moulds the nature and determines the direction of his church. Christ is not only the head, he also gives purpose to the church. In a similar way, Paul describes Christ as the "foundation stone" of the church (I Corinthians 3:10-15). There is no other foundation. Christians must be careful about the quality of their service. They must build a super-structure worthy of the foundation - gold, silver, costly stones, not wood, hay, stubble. Christian service within God's temple, the church, should be active, dedicated, spiritual and of good quality. It is directed by Christ the cornerstone and based on Christ the foundation.

Paul also views the church as

> "built on the foundation of the apostles and prophets, Christ Jesus himself being the cornerstone" (Ephesians 2:20).

For this reason the church is described as "apostolic". The prophets, speaking on God's authority, proclaimed God's Word in the Old Testament. The apostles, acting on Christ's authority, confirmed Christ's work in the New Testament. The links of the church with the Old Testament, however, lie even deeper as the next picture of the church will show.

PEOPLE

All the New Testament writers see the church as people. For them, the church is not a building but people. They describe Christians as brothers and sisters within the family of God. God is their father, they are God's children. The church is God's family.

But the New Testament writers go further defining this family relationship as very special– a relationship of "belonging". The church belongs to God who owns or possesses the church as his own. In the Old Testament this relationship is called a "covenant". A covenant is a solemn agreement between two parties, in which they make promises to each other. Marriage is a covenant between two people, who promise life-long love and faithfulness to each other. God entered into a covenant with his people in the Old Testament, promising to be their God and to care for them and for their children. They promised to be faithful to God, to obey and serve God. The New Testament writers, too, see the church as being in a covenant relationship with God. The church in the New Testament is the continuation of the church in the Old Testament though without the former restriction to the Jewish nation.

Paul sees Gentile Christians as those who, through faith in Jesus the Messiah, have received the blessing of Abraham. They are the "Israel of God". James writes to the twelve tribes scattered among the nations. Peter addresses churches in Asia as God's "elect" dispersed in various areas, sprinkled by Christ's blood, a chosen people, a royal priesthood, a holy nation, a people belonging to God. The writer to the Hebrews prays for his readers the blessing of the God who brought back from the dead our Lord Jesus through the blood of the everlasting covenant. John stresses the Christian's sonship within the covenant family of the church, addressing his readers as children, fathers, young men and friends.

All this teaches us that the writers viewed the church as God's covenant people. What began in the Old Testament people of God, reaching fulfilment in Christ the Messiah, now continues in the New Testament church without racial, social or sexual distinction. And God's covenant of grace is well illustrated in God's covenant people the church. As Christians, we belong to God enjoying, both individually and collectively, a covenant relationship with him.

These pictures of the church are lived out in the story of the Gospels and Acts. Jesus established the church among his disciples. Its foundation was a confession of himself as Messiah and Son of God. Its business was caring for the community based on Christ the Saviour. The Holy Spirit confirmed the existence of the church at Pentecost by coming upon it in power. The spread of the church, which Jesus promised had begun.

Persecution forced the church into Judaea and Samaria. Gentiles entered the church and we see the church grappling with some practical problems at the Jerusalem Council. The church at Antioch commissioned Paul and Barnabas as missionaries. Their journeys led to churches being planted at various centres and a leadership structure established. The web of expansion spread till finally Paul reached Rome.

In all this, we see the church as Christians, grouped in various centres, related to Christ by faith, bonded together in a common salvation, characterised by love. They are branches alive in Christ the vine, members active in Christ the body, a bride in love with Christ the bridegroom, a temple in whose precincts serving God is a priority, a people in covenant relationship with God. Yet they are one, holy, apostolic, catholic or universal church, drawing their membership from every nation, comprising those in every era. Old and New Testament alike. They share faith in one Lord and Saviour, experience one common salvation. They are God's very own people, enjoying God together.

Church is a "means of grace" to the Christian. God provides the Christian with many helps outer and inner, individual and collective. The Christian should neglect none but enjoy them all. This is his privilege as well as his responsibility.

Church

THE PRESBYTERIAN CHURCH

- How does the Presbyterian Church relate to the picture of the church in the New Testament?
- How did the Presbyterian Church begin?
- Where does the Presbyterian Church come from?
- What does the Presbyterian Church believe?

ORIGIN

The Christian church continued, after the period of the apostles, facing various heresies or false teachings and debating at great length the way in which the **two natures of Christ**, the **human** and the **divine**, were to be understood. Eventually, division occurred. The church in the **west** gave allegiance to the bishop of Rome and was known as "**Catholic**". The church in the **east** came under the control of patriarchs and was known as "**Orthodox**".

In the west, during the sixteenth century, the "Reformation" took place. Those protesting against a false teaching on salvation and many practices of the Roman Catholic Church eventually withdrew from that church. In their bid to "reform" or correct the abuses of the Roman Catholic Church they claimed that they were returning to the teaching of scripture and thus became known as "Protestants". At the time of the Reformation a number of groups could be distinguished, each with differing beliefs and practices. These groups help us to understand how our Presbyterian Church came into existence:-

(1) The followers of Martin Luther (1483-1546) formed the Lutheran Church which is the major denomination in Germany, Norway and Sweden.

(2) From John Calvin (1509-1564) came a group of churches which are normally called "Reformed Churches". These took slightly differing forms in various countries. In Scotland and later in Ireland, it was mainly 'Presbyterian'. In England, in the seventeenth century, it became 'Congregational' (Independent).

(3) Various small groups called 'Anabaptists', who rejected

infant baptism and some other beliefs, also arose.

(4) In England, the Reformation had many elements of Calvin's teaching. However, due to the political developments of the day, the "Church of England", not as fully reformed as the continental Churches, came into existence. The figure below indicates the major divisions within Christendom.

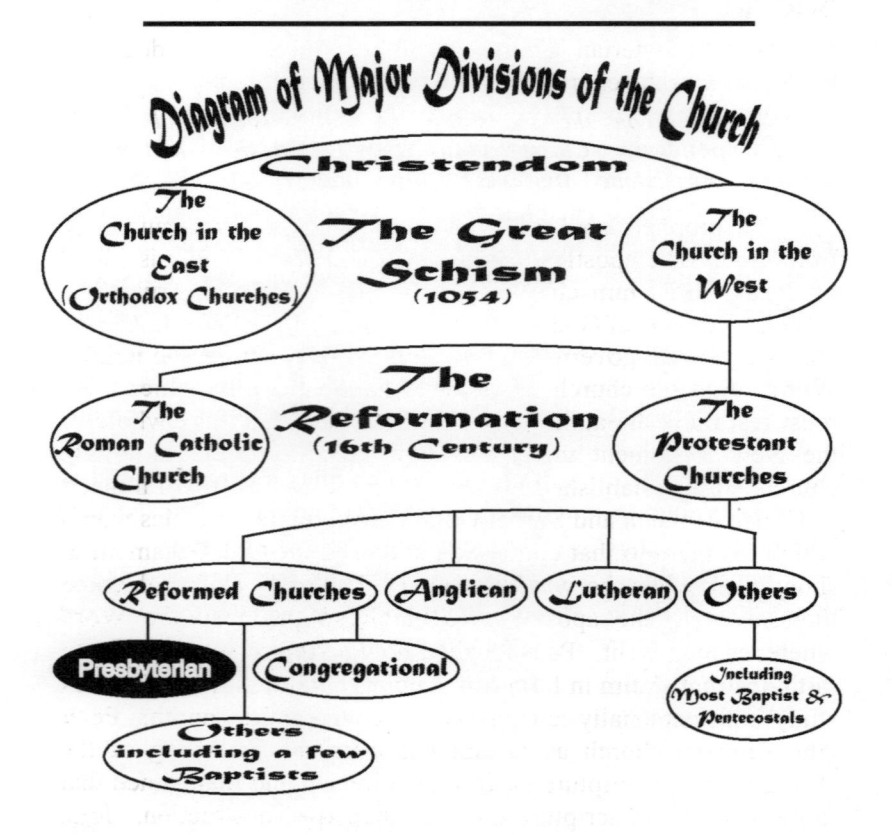

Diagram of Major Divisions of the Church

Christendom — The Great Schism (1054)
- The Church in the East (Orthodox Churches)
- The Church in the West

The Reformation (16th Century)
- The Roman Catholic Church
- The Protestant Churches
  - Reformed Churches
    - Presbyterian
    - Congregational
    - Others including a few Baptists
  - Anglican
  - Lutheran
  - Others (Including Most Baptist & Pentecostals)

CHRISTENDOM

BELIEFS

The Presbyterian Church is part of the "catholic" or world-

Church

wide church of Jesus Christ. It is part of the body of Christ, holding particular views about doctrine and government of the church. These views about doctrine and government are "founded on and agreeable to the "Word of God". The Presbyterian Church is a **biblical church**.

DOCTRINE

The Presbyterian Church is biblical in terms of doctrine. Paul describes the church as

> *"built on the foundation of the apostles and prophets, Christ Jesus himself being the cornerstone"* (Ephesians 2:20).

The prophets spoke to God's people with direct authority from God. The apostles taught, acted and wrote, commissioned by Jesus Christ himself, the head of the church who rules the church by means of God's revealed authority in his Word. Christ, the living Word, governs his church through scripture, the written Word. And the church, in order to have Christ as cornerstone, must rest upon the authority of the Word of God. The whole of the New Testament underlines how basic scripture is to the church. Jesus established his church on the confession of himself as Christ, Messiah and Son of God. He taught his disciples words which led them to that confession and used the Old Testament to show clearly how he was the Christ. The early church devoted themselves to the apostle's teaching and preached the Word wherever they went. Paul recalled how scripture led Timothy to faith, instructed him in faith and should, therefore, be his constant study both personally and in his work within the church. Peter who saw the church as originating from the preaching of the Word, regarded scripture as divinely directed and maintained that those who distort scripture do so to their own destruction. John insisted that to continue in Christ's teaching is to have both the Father and the Son. And the writer to the Hebrews required obedience to God through scripture, because scripture is the living, active and penetrating Word of God.

Clearly, then, the Word of God lies at the very foundation of the church, knowledge of Christ as Saviour and growth in Christ as Head come from this source. Christ, as Head, establishes and develops his church through the Word.

> *"The word of God, which consists of the Scriptures of the Old and New Testaments, is the only rule to direct us how to glorify and enjoy him"* (S.C. 2).

SUBORDINATE STANDARDS

The Subordinate Standards of the Presbyterian Church in Ireland are the Shorter and Larger Catechisms and the Westminster Confession of Faith. These documents were written in the seventeenth century at Westminster in London during the period after the Reformation. The subordinate standards are meant to declare what she believes scripture teaches on certain important matters of faith and practice.

Most of us should know the Shorter Catechism already quoted in our study. Through questions and answers, it explains what the Bible teaches about itself as the Word of God, about God who controls everything and who provides a covenant plan to save man from sin, about Jesus Christ, God's Son, who puts this plan into action and about how a person becomes a Christian and develops in the Christian life. The Larger Catechism, also in question and answer form, gives fuller answers to these questions. The Westminster Confession of Faith contains thirty-three chapters, which are statements of what the Bible teaches on important themes connected with faith. The Confession of Faith includes all the subjects dealt with in the Catechisms but adds some others.

The Catechisms and Confession of Faith are all "subordinate standards", that is, they are "under" or "beneath" the authority of Scripture, never claiming to be the Word of God or "inspired" like the Bible. They may contain errors. The Subordinate Standards seek to set out, as clearly as possible, what the Bible teaches on certain important matters of Christian faith and practice. For this reason, there are "proof-texts" of scripture references for statements in the Subordinate Standards.

Church

GOVERNMENT

The Presbyterian Church also claims to be biblical in government. Not only what she believes but how she functions as a church is "founded on and agreeable to the Word of God". In the Bible there is no precise blue-print of how she should work as a church but there are principles which can help direct or regulate how she works. At the time of the founding of the Presbyterian Church in the seventeenth century, these principles were set out in a document called, "The form of Presbyterian Church Government".

Elder

The key to understanding this form of church government is the name "Presbyterian". Presbyterian comes from the New Testament word PRESBYTER. Presbyter means "elder". The Presbyterian Church is a church governed by elders meeting in presbytery.

Since the Presbyterian Church claims that her government is based on the Bible, the place of the presbyter or elder, as a leader within the church, must be very important and, when we examine the evidence in the Bible, we find that this is so. In the Old Testament (Exodus 18) elders had a leading role to play among God's people and, turning to the New Testament church, we find they have an equally important place.

Elders received gifts, which they brought to the Jerusalem Church. Elders discussed with the apostles how Gentile Christians were to be admitted to the church. After Paul had planted churches in Asia and had returned to strengthen these new Christians, he appointed elders to look after them. Paul told Titus to appoint elders in Crete as a vital step to help offset matters lacking in church life there. Clearly, therefore, elders were important in establishing and developing new Christians in their faith.

In the New Testament "bishop" is the same office as elder.

Paul called the elders of Ephesus to meet him at Miletus and, when speaking to them, addressed them as "bishops". Paul directed Titus to appoint elders in every town in Crete and then, as though referring to the same office immediately went on to give the qualifications of a "bishop". Elders are bishops.

What did elders do? What was their work? One thing they did was to "govern" or "rule" the church – leadership was their function. While not dictatorial, nor oppressive, it was none-the-less leadership. They were set over God's people to direct the church. As parents bring up their children in the family, elders were to help Christians grow in their faith. Elders were to be highly respected in the church and, only on the firmest evidence, were accusations to be brought against them.

Teaching was another part of the elder's work. Indeed, there are good grounds for seeing all elders as involved in leadership, some given the particular task of teaching. Paul writes to Timothy,

> *"Let the elders who rule well be considered worthy of double honour, especially those who labour in preaching and teaching."* (I Timothy 5:17).

This is why, today, the minister is sometimes referred to as "teaching elder" and members of Kirk Session as "ruling elders".

In the New Testament this leadership is called "oversight" or "superintendency" and is viewed as something warm and loving, for elders are to care for the church as the shepherd looks after his sheep

> *"Pay careful attention to yourselves and to all the flock, in which the Holy Spirit has made you overseers, to care for the church of God, which he obtained with his own blood"* (Acts 20:28).

Church

This bidding is particularly tender, when we remember how Jesus describes himself as the good shepherd, who genuinely cares for his sheep and eventually displays that care by dying for them.

Peter reminded elders to carry out their work in the proper spirit, as under-shepherds, looking to Christ the Chief Shepherd. Paul told the Ephesian elders to feed the flock, guarding them against wolves who distort the truth. James declared that sick folk should call for the elders of the church to pray for them and to anoint them with oil in the Lord's name. By ruling, teaching and pastoring God's flock, presbyters or elders carry out a vital leadership function in the church.

Deacon

Elders' duties were mainly to do with teaching and developing Christians in their faith, but there were other aspects to the early church's life and work. Christians cared practically for one another. When a dispute arose over money allocation to Greek and Hebrew widows, the apostles realised how time-consuming a problem it could be, decided, as a priority to devote themselves to the word and prayer. But asked the church to appoint seven men to look after this matter of finance and caring.

> *"Now in these days when the disciples were increasing in number, a complaint by the Hellenists arose against the Hebrews because their widows were being neglected in the daily distribution. And the twelve summoned the full number of the disciples and said, 'It is not right that we should give up preaching the word of God to serve tables. Therefore, brothers, pick out from among you seven men of good repute, full of the Spirit and of wisdom, whom we will appoint to this duty. But we will devote ourselves to prayer and to the ministry of the word.' And what they said pleased the whole gathering, and they chose Stephen, a man full of faith*

> and of the Holy Spirit, and Philip, and Prochorus, and Nicanor, and Timon, and Parmenas, and Nicolaus, a proselyte of Antioch. These they set before the apostles, and they prayed and laid their hands on them" (Acts 6:1-6).
>
> "Deacons likewise must be dignified, not double-tongued, not addicted to much wine, not greedy for dishonest gain. They must hold the mystery of the faith with a clear conscience. And let them also be tested first; then let them serve as deacons if they prove themselves blameless. Their wives likewise must be dignified, not slanderers, but sober-minded, faithful in all things. Let deacons each be the husband of one wife, managing their children and their own households well. For those who serve well as deacons gain a good standing for themselves and also great confidence in the faith that is in Christ Jesus" (I Timothy 3:8-13).

Later, in the New Testament, when we read of the qualifications for "deacons", integrity and ability in practical financial affairs are found to be essential. Presbyterians tend to see the "deacons" of Paul's letters as a development of the "Seven" in Acts 6 whose work within the church consists of practical care and dealing with financial matters. We try to reflect the division between elders and deacons in the distinction between the work of the Kirk Session and that of the Congregational Committee. Kirk Session or elders look after "spiritual oversight" whereas the Congregational Committee as "deacons", look after "temporal matters" such as practical care and finance.

PRESBYTERIAN

From this we can see what makes us different in our church government as a Presbyterian Church from other denominations. "Episcopal" churches like the Church of England/Ireland have three ranks of "ministry"- bishop, priest, deacon, as compared with the two tiers in our system - elders and deacons.

Church

"Congregational" or "independent" churches, in many cases today, have elders but these are subject ultimately to the church meeting of local believers and function only within the local church, not beyond it. As Presbyterians, we believe that elders' rule and leadership extends beyond the local congregation to the whole church. So as well as our Kirk Session, we have our Presbytery, Synod and General Assembly. These church courts extend government by elders beyond the local congregation. We see the principle involved here as evident in the Jerusalem Council in Acts 15, where a decision reached by the apostles and elders of the Jerusalem Church affected the Church at Antioch.

What Presbyterians are seeking to do, above all, is to have a form of church government based on the principles of God's Word. In doctrine and government, our Presbyterian Church is "founded on and agreeable to the Word of God". We have to develop our Presbyterian Church from the picture of the church in the Bible. As a Christian, you can look forward to developing your Christian life within the fellowship of the Presbyterian Church.

SUMMARY

Church

THE CHURCH AND HER HEAD

THE VINE

1. What truth about the Church is expressed in the picture of the vine in John 15?

   _____

   _____

THE BODY

2. What two basic truths about the Church are suggested in this picture of the Church as the body of Christ?

   _____

   cf. Romans 12:4-8 and I Corinthians 12:12-31

   _____

   cf. Ephesians 4:11-16

THE BRIDE

3. What does the illustration of marriage teach about the relationship between Christ and the Church?

   _____

   _____

   cf. Ephesians 5:22-33

THE TEMPLE

4. Can you suggest some of the implications of being a holy priesthood in God's Temple (See I Peter 2:4, 5, 9, 10)

   _____

Church

_____
_____

PEOPLE

5. In your own words how would you describe the special relationship between God and His people?

_____
_____
_____
_____

THE PRESBYTERIAN CHURCH

ORIGIN

1. Which particular reformer is regarded as the "father" of the Reformed Churches?

_____

BELIEFS

2. Who is the head of the Church?

_____

3. How does God primarily reveal His will to the Church?

_____

4. In your own words, what are the benefits of the subordinate standards of the Presbyterian Church?

_____
_____

5. How is the Presbyterian Church governed?

_____

6. What is the distinction between the ruling and the teaching elder?

7. From 1 Peter 5:1-4 what should be the attitude of an elder?

8. In your own words, what is the distinctive feature of Presbyterian Church government?

CHAPTER 6
SACRAMENTS

God provides many helps for the Christian. These, as we have seen, are called the "means of grace". The "inner" means are justification, adoption and sanctification. The "outer" means include the Word of God, prayer, fellowship and the church. The Shorter Catechism specifically mentions another means of grace - the sacraments –

> *"The outward and ordinary means whereby Christ communicateth to us the benefits of redemption, are his ordinances, especially the Word, sacraments, and prayer; all of which are made effectual to the elect for salvation"* (S.C. 88).
>
> © "Confession of Faith and Subordinate Standards" The Free Church of Scotland

We come now to study the sacraments, a further help for the Christian to grow in grace.

The word "sacrament" does not occur in the Bible but it is a very helpful word, explaining an important teaching which occurs in the Bible. The word sacrament comes from the Latin word SACRAMENTUM meaning an "oath" or "promise". The Roman soldier swore a SACRAMENTUM or oath of allegiance to Caesar. A sacrament is a reminder of the promises which God makes with his people in the covenant of grace. It is a visual aid to help us see more clearly what God does in salvation, symbol of God's promise of salvation. It is a seal affirming God's authority to bring about salvation. A sacrament is a sign or seal of the covenant of grace.

God gave signs and seals to his people in Old Testament days. God gave Noah a rainbow, a reminder of God's promise that he would never destroy the earth again by a flood. God gave Abraham circumcision, a reminder of God's promise to be his God and a God to his children. God gave Moses the Passover Feast, a reminder of the miraculous way in which God had rescued his people from slavery in Egypt.

What Presbyterians Believe

God continued to give signs and seals of his promises to his people in the New Testament. Christ introduced baptism and the Lord's Supper.

> *"Go therefore and make disciples of all nations, baptizing them in the name of the Father and of the Son and of the Holy Spirit"* (Matthew 28:19).

> *"Now as they were eating, Jesus took bread, and after blessing it broke it and gave it to the disciples, and said, 'Take, eat; this is my body.' And he took a cup, and when he had given thanks he gave it to them, saying, 'Drink of it, all of you, for this is my blood of the covenant, which is poured out for many for the forgiveness of sins'"* (Matthew 26:26-28).

In this way, Christ commanded his people to observe baptism and the Lord's Supper. The remainder of the New Testament recalls how the early church continued to do this.

Indeed, the New Testament teaches that not only did God continue to give signs through Jesus' teaching as He had done in Old Testament days, but that God fulfilled Old Testament signs in those signs which Jesus gave. Thus, baptism is the New Testament counterpart of circumcision and the Lord's Supper replaces the Passover Feast. This is certainly the way Paul views these signs and writes about them (I Corinthians 10:1-4; I Corinthians 5:7; Romans 15:8; Colossians 2:11, 12).

Baptism and the Lord's Supper are "sensible" signs, that is, signs capable of being appreciated through the senses of sight, touch and taste. They are signs of how God in salvation washes away our sins and then helps us to grow in the Christian life, nourished through feeding on Christ by faith. Baptism and the Lord's Supper are sacraments of "entrance into" and "nourishment within" the Christian life.

The Shorter Catechism's definition of a sacrament is very clear,

> *"A sacrament is an holy ordinance appointed by*

Sacraments

> *Christ, by which, by visible signs, Christ and the benefits of the new covenant, are represented, sealed and applied to believers"* (S.C. 92).

This also makes it clear that there is nothing in the sacrament itself or in the person carrying out the sacrament which makes it an effective help. The help comes from God's promises only through faith in Christ.

> *"The sacraments become effectual means of salvation, not from any virtue, in them, or in him that doth administer them; but only by the blessing of Christ, and the working of the Spirit in them that by faith receive them"* (S.C. 91).

© "Confession of Faith and Subordinate Standards" The Free Church of Scotland

There is nothing automatic or magical about sacraments. They have no value in and of themselves. They are simple, yet meaningful, signs and seals of God's promises in the covenant of grace. God's plan of salvation. They help Christians grasp more firmly and clearly God's promises of salvation. The water remains water in baptism. The water does not wash away our sins. The bread and wine remain bread and wine in the Lord's Supper. The bread and wine do not feed us spiritually. They are all signs pointing to what God does for us when we obey the gospel. They are seals reminding us of God's authority alone to do these things for the believer.

Since a sacrament is *"an holy ordinance, instituted by Christ"* (S.C. 92), there are only two sacraments in the New Testament,

> *"The sacraments of the New Testament are two only, Baptism and the Lord's Supper [and these take the place of Circumcision and the Passover in the Old Testament]"* (S.C. 93).

The Lord's Supper is also called "Communion", "Breaking of Bread" and is known, especially in unreformed churches, as the "Eucharist" or "Mass". The Roman Catholic Church teaches that there are seven sacraments, adding five to the two already mentioned. Confirmation, Penance, Ordination, Marriage and

Extreme Unction. We disagree with this, since there is no evidence of Christ instituting these five. The Roman Catholic Church also teaches that grace or salvation is conferred by the sacraments "through their own work" (EX OPERE OPERATO) and not by faith alone. We also disagree with this. Sacraments are only signs and seals of God's promise of salvation. They are not necessary for salvation. Salvation does not come through them.

BAPTISM

The meaning of baptism can be seen vividly in the New Testament. There are a number of helpful pictures here.

CLEANSING FROM SIN

Baptism depicts cleansing from sin. This comes from the use of water and the idea of washing associated with baptism. A good example of this is when Ananias urged Paul to be baptised.

> "And now why do you wait? Rise and be baptized and wash away your sins, calling on his name." (Acts 22:16).

UNION WITH CHRIST

Baptism portrays union with Christ. Paul reminds the Christians both in Rome and in Colosse that they have been buried with Christ through baptism into his death and are now alive through Christ's resurrection.

> "We were buried therefore with him by baptism into death, in order that, just as Christ was raised from the dead by the glory of the Father, we too might walk in newness of life" (Romans 6:4; Colossians 2:11, 12).

ADMISSION TO THE CHURCH

Baptism symbolises becoming a member of the church, the body of Christ. While Paul has the inner meaning in view, as he writes to the Corinthians, the outer sign emphasises the meaning.

> "For in one Spirit we were all baptized into one body– Jews or Greeks, slaves or free . . ." (I Corinthians 12:13).

Sacraments

Those baptised on the day of Pentecost were added to the church

> *"So those who received his word were baptized, and there were added that day about three thousand souls"* (Acts 2:41).

COVENANT OF GRACE

Baptism signifies the covenant of grace. Paul links baptism with the covenant of grace in two places particularly. He describes the Colossian Christians as both circumcised by Christ and baptised into Christ

> *"In him also you were circumcised with a circumcision made without hands, by putting off the body of the flesh, by the circumcision of Christ, having been buried with him in baptism, in which you were also raised with him through faith in the powerful working of God, who raised him from the dead"* (Colossians 2:11, 12).

He tells the Galatian Christians that those who were baptised into Christ have been clothed with Christ and that those who belong to Christ *"are Abraham's seed and heirs according to the promise"* (Galatians 3:27, 29). The Shorter Catechism sums up the meaning of baptism like this.

> "Baptism is the sacrament [of solemn admission into the church on earth] in which the washing with water in the name of the Father, and of the Son, and of the Holy Spirit, signifies and seals our being grafted into Christ, our having a share in the benefits of the covenant of grace, and our pledge to be the Lord's" (S.C. 94).

Christians differ as to who should be baptised. The Baptist Church and others believe that only adults should be baptised on their own profession of faith. The Presbyterian Church among others teaches that baptism is not only for believers but also for their children. The Shorter Catechism states,

> "Baptism is not to be administered to any outside membership of the church on earth, until they profess their faith in Christ and obedience to him; but infants descending from parents (one or both)

> *professing faith in Christ and obedience to him, [are, for that reason, within the covenant and] are to be baptised"* (S.C. 95).

The baptism of children of believers is called Infant Baptism or Paedo-baptism from the Greek word PAIS meaning child.

Presbyterians believe that people who are not Christians ought not to be baptised until they become Christians, that is, until they *"profess their faith in Christ and obedience to him"*. Peter urged those who were cut to the heart because of their sin, to repent and be baptised

> *"And Peter said to them, 'Repent and be baptized every one of you in the name of Jesus Christ for the forgiveness of your sins, and you will receive the gift of the Holy Spirit . . .'"* (Acts 2:38).

Presbyterians also believe that the child of a Christian parent ought to be baptised because baptism is a sign and seal of the covenant of grace. People often have wrong ideas about baptism. Some think it is a ceremony which gives the child a name, others that it will make the child thrive and many feel that it is the proper thing to do for every child. Some refer to it as "christening" believing that it automatically makes a child a Christian. **None of these ideas is true.**

There is one covenant of grace or plan of salvation in the Bible. The covenant of grace contains the basic principle that the promise of salvation is for the believer and for his children. Children of believers were included in the covenant in the Old Testament and received the covenant sign of circumcision. The principle continues in the New Testament since Peter maintains that the promise is for those repenting of sin and for their children, while Paul insists that the child of one believing parent is "holy"

> *"For the unbelieving husband is made holy because of his wife, and the unbelieving wife is made holy because of her husband. Otherwise your children would be unclean, but as it is, they are holy"* (I Corinthians 7:14; Acts 2:38).

Sacraments

Baptism has replaced circumcision as a sign of the covenant of grace. Both circumcision and baptism are essentially signs of the same thing, namely, salvation. The identification of these two signs can be seen when Paul describes Christians as circumcised by Christ and baptised into Christ (Colossians 2:11-13). Baptism is related to the covenant with Abraham

> *"For as many of you as were baptized into Christ have put on Christ. There is neither Jew nor Greek, there is neither slave nor free, there is no male and female, for you are all one in Christ Jesus. And if you are Christ's, then you are Abraham's offspring, heirs according to promise"* (Galatians 3:27-29).

Paul uses the signs of the covenant interchangeably, referring to baptism and the Lord's Supper, when speaking of the church in the Old Testament[1] and to the Passover and circumcision, when speaking of the church in the New Testament [2]

Baptism is therefore to be administered on the same principle as circumcision was, to adults who become believers and to the children of believers. This is why there are instances in the New Testament not only of individuals being baptised, for example, the Ethiopian eunuch (Acts 8:38) and Paul (Acts 9:18) but also of family baptisms, for example, the family of Lydia (Acts 16:15), of the Philippian jailer (Acts 16:33) and of Stephanas (I Corinthians 1:16).

When a child is baptised God is declaring that the child is

---

[1] *"For I want you to know, brothers, that our fathers were all under the cloud, and all passed through the sea, and all were baptized into Moses in the cloud and in the sea, and all ate the same spiritual food, and all drank the same spiritual drink. For they drank from the spiritual Rock that followed them, and the Rock was Christ"* (I Corinthians 10:1-4).

[2] *"Cleanse out the old leaven that you may be a new lump, as you really are unleavened. For Christ, our Passover lamb, has been sacrificed"* (I Corinthians 5:7; Romans 15:8; Colossians 2:11, 12).

special to Him. Although salvation is promised, in time the child must come to God and by faith acknowledge Jesus Christ as Lord and Saviour.

When a child is baptised parents are declaring openly that they are Christians and that they want their child to come to know Jesus Christ in a personal way and to grow up to serve Him. They are asking for God's help and the support of the Church as they bring up their child in the ways of Christ.

Presbyterians do not believe that immersion is necessary for baptism.

> "Dipping of the person into the water is not necessary. Baptism is rightly administered by pouring or sprinkling water on the person"
> (W.C. 28:3).

The **Greek words** for **baptise** do **not mean exclusively to immerse** in the New Testament. Cases which appear to prove immersion are inconclusive. Pouring is an apt symbol of the coming of God's Spirit upon a person. Sprinkling was the main Old Testament mode of ceremonial purification and the Greek word for baptism is used to describe this in the New Testament (Hebrews 9:10).

Baptism is a vivid symbol of cleansing from sin, of union with Christ, of admission to the church and of the covenant of grace. As a sign and seal of the covenant of grace it is meaningfully administered to believers and to their children. Pouring or sprinkling effectively portrays the coming of the Spirit or the cleansing from sin depicted by the sacrament.

When we see the plan of salvation in the Bible as a covenant of grace beginning in the Old Testament finding fulfilment in Jesus Christ the mediator of the covenant and continuing in the New Testament, when we accept baptism and the Lord's Supper as covenant signs and seals replacing circumcision and the Passover, it helps us understand better our position on the sacraments and makes Infant Baptism a meaningful and biblical representation of the covenant of grace.

Sacraments

We need always to remember, however, that as sacraments baptism and the Lord's Supper are "outer signs" of an "inner grace". Baptism never confers grace. The status of the covenant child is not of one who is automatically a Christian because of the covenant but rather of one to whom the promise of salvation is particularly offered because of the covenant. What is offered in grace must be received personally by faith. Infant baptism anticipates a time when the child will receive Christ as Lord and Saviour by personal faith.

LORD'S SUPPER

The origins of the Lord's Supper are described in the gospels of Matthew, Mark and Luke. Its place in the history of the church is mentioned in Acts. An instance of its observance is noted in Paul's first letter to the Corinthians. As we examine this material, certain striking characteristics of the Lord's Supper emerge.

REMEMBRANCE

The Lord's Supper involves remembrance of a dying Saviour. Jesus' words introducing the meal to his disciples are important here, *"Do this in remembrance of me"* (Luke 22:19; I Corinthians 11:24). The form of the bread and wine is also significant. The bread was broken, recalling Christ's body crucified on the cross. The wine was poured out, a reminder of Christ's shed blood. Together the bread and wine speak of the finality of Christ's once for all sacrifice (Hebrews 9:28).

COMMUNION

The Lord's Supper implies communion with a living Lord. Christ is risen from death and is alive for evermore. We converse and share our thoughts with him in the present. "Memory is absence felt, communion is presence realised". We can, of course, have communion with Christ at any time or in any place. The communion service does not offer anything more of Christ than we have on any occasion when the Word is preached.

The setting suggests nourishment. The idea of the meal means not only fellowship with Christ but feeding on him. We refresh our spirits and renew our faith by meeting with Christ and drawing on the resources of his strength.

> *"The cup of blessing that we bless, is it not a participation in the blood of Christ? The bread that we break, is it not a participation in the body of Christ?"* (I Corinthians 10:16).

This is "spiritual" feeding and all ideas of "physical" activity must be avoided.

The setting also suggests witness. The Lord's Supper is an opportunity for those who share a common salvation to affirm their faith publicly. Paul writes,

> *"For as often as you eat this bread and drink the cup, you proclaim the Lord's death until he comes"* (I Corinthians 11:26).

The word for "proclaim" means, literally, to "announce good news", to "evangelise". The Lord's Supper is a way for Christians to show how much they think of Christ's death and thus to proclaim the good news to others.

ANTICIPATION

The Lord's Supper anticipates a coming Judge,

> *"For as often as you eat this bread and drink the cup, you proclaim the Lord's death until he comes"* (I Corinthians 11:26).

For the unbeliever, the prospect of Christ's return is one of condemnation and judgment. For the believer, it means vindication and joy around the Lord's Table as the bride of Christ. The Church anticipates the wedding reception of Christ the bridegroom

> *"And the angel said to me, 'Write this: Blessed are those who are invited to the marriage supper of the*

Sacraments

> Lamb.' And he said to me, 'These are the true words of God'" (Revelation 19:9).

COVENANT OF GRACE

Like baptism, the Lord's Supper is a sign and seal of the covenant of grace. Indeed, it replaces the Old Testament sign of the Passover meal. Jesus introduced the Lord's Supper on the occasion of the Passover. He specifically remarked,

> ". . . *this is my blood of the covenant, which is poured out for many for the forgiveness of sins"* (Matthew 26:28).

Paul described Christ as "our Passover lamb" and urged Christians at Corinth to live ". . . *not with the old yeast, the yeast of malice and wickedness, but with bread without yeast, the bread of sincerity and truth"* (I Corinthians 5:7, 8). Just as believers in the Old Testament recalled redemption from Egyptian slavery through the Passover Feast, so believers in the New Testament recall redemption from sin in the Lord's Supper. But in the latter the blood of a greater Lamb is remembered. The Shorter Catechism states,

> *"The Lord's Supper is a sacrament in which, by giving and receiving bread and wine according to Christ's appointment, his death is proclaimed, and those who receive rightly are by faith (and not by the mouth in a physical manner) made partakers of his body and blood, with all his benefits, to their spiritual nourishment and growth in grace"* (S.C. 96).

The question as to who should take part in the Lord's Supper is just as important as the matter of who should be baptised. The Shorter Catechism explains the meaning of each sacrament but also indicates the persons to whom each sacrament correctly applies.

> *"It is required of those who would receive rightly the Lord's Supper, that they examine themselves as to their knowledge of the meaning and object of this sacrament, their faith to feed upon Christ, and their repentance, love and new obedience; for*

coming in an unworthy manner would bring judgment on themselves" (S.C. 97).

Scripture is quite clear in its warning on this aspect.

> *"Let a person examine himself, then, and so eat of the bread and drink of the cup. For anyone who eats and drinks without discerning the body eats and drinks judgment on himself"* (I Corinthians 11:28, 29).

This arises naturally from the setting and nature of the Lord's Supper. Disciples, who were already totally committed to Jesus as Messiah and Lord ate the meal in the first instance. The meaning of the Lord's Supper further clarifies the issue. Only those who have known conversion to Christ through repentance and faith can effectively remember Christ's death. Only those who have had the barrier of sin removed can commune with Christ, feed on him and meaningfully witness to the power of his death. Only those who have experienced justification, adoption and sanctification can anticipate Christ's return with glad eagerness. The covenant sign of the Lord's Supper is for God's covenant people, for those capable of *"discerning the body of the Lord"* and its significance for their own lives personally.

Baptism, the **"sacrament of entrance"**, depicts cleansing from sin, union with Christ and admission to the church. The Lord's Supper, the **"sacrament of nourishment"**, implies remembrance of a dying Saviour, communion with a living Lord and anticipation of a coming Judge. Both are signs and seals of the covenant of grace. God's plan of salvation. Baptism replaces circumcision. The Lord's Supper replaces the Passover. God signifies and seals his promises in this way.

COMMUNICANT MEMBERSHIP

As signs and seals of the covenant of grace the sacraments of baptism and the Lord's Supper are great helps to the Christian. They depict entry into and continuation within the Christian life in visual form. They assure the Christian of Christ's sufficiency

Sacraments

both for justification and sanctification. They recall God's sovereignty not only in initiating but in effectively carrying out and completing salvation. They remind the Christian of the promises of God behind the covenant of grace.

In the case of baptism, sadly, this has not always been so. Bitter disputes among Christians as to who should be baptised and as to what form baptism ought to take have often obscured the glory of this great ordinance. Within Presbyterian circles, ignorance, misunderstanding and improper administration of baptism has produced confusion, heartache and hurt.

The Presbyterian Church recognises two kinds of "members" associated with the church. There are those who attend services, send their children to Sunday School and youth organisations, support the work financially but, though interested, have not yet come to faith in Christ or to a public profession of faith in Christ. They are described as "adherents". They are like the "unbelievers" or "inquirers" whom Paul describes at Corinth

> *"If, therefore, the whole church comes together and all speak in tongues, and outsiders or unbelievers enter, will they not say that you are out of your minds? But if all prophesy, and an unbeliever or outsider enters, he is convicted by all, he is called to account by all"* (I Corinthians 14:23, 24).

The other kind of member is a "full" or "communicant member". They have come to faith in Christ and have become communicant or full members of the church. They are like those on the day of Pentecost, who heard Peter preach the gospel, were concerned about being sinners, repented of sin, believed in Christ as Saviour, were baptised and were added to the church. Such people are described as "saved"

> *"Let all the house of Israel therefore know for certain that God has made him both Lord and Christ, this Jesus whom you crucified."*

103

> *Now when they heard this they were cut to the heart, and said to Peter and the rest of the apostles, 'Brothers, what shall we do?' And Peter said to them, 'Repent and be baptized every one of you in the name of Jesus Christ for the forgiveness of your sins, and you will receive the gift of the Holy Spirit. For the promise is for you and for your children and for all who are far off, everyone whom the Lord our God calls to himself.' And with many other words he bore witness and continued to exhort them, saying, 'Save yourselves from this crooked generation.' So those who received his word were baptized, and there were added that day about three thousand souls"* (Acts 2:36-41).
>
> *". . . praising God and having favor with all the people. And the Lord added to their number day by day those who were being saved"* (Acts 2:47).

The Presbyterian Church admits people to full or communicant membership on profession of faith in Christ and *requires that they have been baptised.* Communicant or church membership classes are specifically designed to deal with this matter. Taking the Lord's Supper, like baptism, rightly requires a profession of faith.

In the classes, instruction is given on the nature of a profession of faith, on the sacraments of baptism and the Lord's Supper and on the implications of communicant membership. This is designed to lead to a public profession of faith and becoming a communicant member.

> A public profession of faith includes an affirmation of personal faith in Christ as Saviour through repentance and faith, a declared intention of continuing in the Christian life and a promise to use the *"means of grace"* and to be a faithful member of the church.

This public profession must be "credible" or "believable".

Sacraments

Our way of life and interest in the means of grace and in the church must demonstrate the sincerity of our profession. A credible profession of faith is not just a belief in the general idea of Christian teaching, nor simply a statement that you accept Christian doctrine, nor merely a matter of form so that you can take part in the sacrament. It is a sincere profession of personal saving faith in Christ. Its public nature is demonstrated through answers to questions asked and promises made before Kirk Session at Pre-Communion or Communion service.

The issues dealt with in these lessons reach their climax here:
- Have I responded to God's call in the gospel?
- Have I experienced conversion through repentance and faith?
- Am I justified and adopted by God?
- Has sanctification begun in my life?
- Is there evidence of salvation in my life to which I can point?
- Am I a Christian?

> When we can honestly answer "yes" to these questions, we have fulfilled the basic requirements of communicant membership in a profession of faith.

If we cannot respond with "yes" to these questions, we must not proceed to communicant membership. To do so would be a failure to *"recognise the body of the Lord"*. In this way the lessons help us to examine ourselves in order to see if we are in the faith.

Communicant membership, then, is not a matter of form. It arises from the very personal nature of the covenant of grace. It requires a worthy response and a sincere consideration of the covenant signs and seals, the sacraments of baptism and the Lord's Supper. Only such an approach will ensure worthy reception, for worthiness lies in felt unworthiness and in turning to Christ personally for salvation.

SUMMARY

SACRAMENTS

1. In your own words, "What is a Sacrament?"

2. What two Sacraments did Christ introduce to the Church? (Matthew 28:19 and Matthew 26:26, 27)

3. What was the Old Testament equivalent of these two Sacraments?

BAPTISM

1. What does Baptism signify?

2. What does the Presbyterian Church believe about who is eligible for baptism?

3. What are parents declaring as they present their child for baptism?

Sacraments

_____
_____

THE LORD'S SUPPER

1. What is being remembered in the Sacrament of the Lord's Supper? (Luke 22:19, 20)

   _____
   _____

2. What is the significance of the word "communion"?

   _____
   _____
   _____

3. What event does the Lord's Supper anticipate? (Revelation 19:9)

   _____

4. Who should participate in the Lord's Supper?

   _____
   _____

COMMUNICANT MEMBERSHIP

In your own words describe the difference between an adherent and a communicant member in the Presbyterian Church.

_____
_____
_____

CHAPTER 7

CHRISTIAN LIFE

It is clear by now in our study that communicant membership is not a matter of form. It is for those who have a saving knowledge of Christ. Reception into full church membership through a public profession of faith in Christ as Saviour and Lord is not an end in itself. It is a means to an end, namely, living the Christian life. The Bible helps us to see how being a Christian affects every part of our lives. It does this by stressing certain areas where Christ's kingly rule over us should be particularly evident. We need to study these areas in detail.

PERSONAL

Christ's kingdom is intensely personal. Jesus emphasises growth as a result of his rule in the Christian's life. He uses the picture of the vine to teach this lesson (John 15:1-8). Jesus is the vine. God is the gardener. We are the branches. We only have life as we are joined to Christ the vine and the entire purpose of our existence is to grow as branches and to produce fruit. God prunes the branches for that very reason. Fruitless branches are useless. They are cut off, thrown away and burned. Growth and fruit bearing for the Christian are essential. They are his reason for existence.

Paul helps us to understand the nature of this growth. He describes the growth as "fruit of the Spirit". He itemises the fruit in detail.

> *"But the fruit of the Spirit is love, joy, peace, patience, kindness, goodness, faithfulness, gentleness, self-control"* (Galatians 5:22).

Notice how the fruit are marks of character. They refer to the kind of people we become as Christians. They describe a changed human nature. Paul contrasts,

> *"the fruit of the Spirit"* with *"the acts of the sinful nature"* (Galatians 5:19, 22). (NIV)

Peter stresses the development of this growth II Peter 1:5-11.

> *"For this very reason, make every effort to supplement your faith with virtue, and virtue with knowledge, and knowledge with self-control, and self-control with steadfastness, and steadfastness with godliness, and godliness with brotherly affection, and brotherly affection with love. For if these qualities are yours and are increasing, they keep you from being ineffective or unfruitful in the knowledge of our Lord Jesus Christ. For whoever lacks these qualities is so nearsighted that he is blind, having forgotten that he was cleansed from his former sins. Therefore, brothers, be all the more diligent to make your calling and election sure, for if you practice these qualities you will never fall. For in this way there will be richly provided for you an entrance into the eternal kingdom of our Lord and Savior Jesus Christ"* (II Peter 1: 5-11).

Again, these refer to character. The presence of such qualities in increasing measure indicates Christian productivity. Their absence suggests spiritual blindness and forgetfulness.

> *"For whoever lacks these qualities is so nearsighted that he is blind, having forgotten that he was cleansed from his former sins"* (II Peter 1:9).

It is obvious from this, that personal growth and fruit bearing in character are an essential, natural and on-going part of Christian living, not an optional extra. The remarkable thing is that spiritual rebirth produces such effective changes in our lives. By these things, we recognise that we are Christians and, through them, we ourselves gain assurance of salvation. The problem is, how does this come about? Is there anything we ought to be doing to stimulate this growth and development?

There is, and the key to personal growth is in obedience to Christ. Jesus teaches that, as branches, we ought to "abide" or

Christian Life

"remain" in him the vine. He also indicates how we might do this.

> *"If you abide in me, and my words abide in you, ask whatever you wish, and it will be done for you. By this my Father is glorified, that you bear much fruit and so prove to be my disciples"* (John 15:7, 8).

Therefore the way to, continuing obedience in Christ, lies in the Word and prayer. Prayer and the Word are vital to the Christian not only privately in his own devotions or "quiet time" but corporately in both Lord's Day services, Mid-week Fellowship and prayer meetings. All of these are a "must" for the Christian for growth in grace. When any of these is neglected or devalued, growth is threatened and character building imperilled. We remain in Christ through the Word and prayer, individually and corporately, and this practical obedience further transforms character.

Paul helps us further along the road of obedience to Christ. He describes obedience to Christ as dying to an old nature and living in a new way. Paul contrasts the acts of the sinful nature with the fruit of the Spirit. Christians have crucified the sinful nature with its passions and desires. They are led by the Spirit, live by the Spirit and keep in step with the Spirit.

This involves the Christian in a deliberate life-style. There are attitudes and actions he will destroy. There are activities and behaviour he will encourage and develop. Obedience to Christ will mean tracing out the pattern of Christ's death and resurrection in his life. Dead to sin and alive to righteousness, he will try to live in this way. He will study the Bible to direct him as to what he must destroy and as to what he must encourage. He will pray to God to help him in this. Obedience to Christ will involve him in daily repentance, as he turns from sin and death to Christ and life. In this way, he will follow Christ and Christ will be more and more patterned in his life.

Peter stresses the effort involved in obedience to Christ.

"For this very reason, make every effort to supplement your faith with virtue, and virtue with knowledge," (II Peter 1:5).

"Therefore, brothers, be all the more diligent to make your calling and election sure, for if you practice these qualities you will never fall. For in this way there will be richly provided for you an entrance into the eternal kingdom of our Lord and Savior Jesus Christ" (II Peter 1:10, 11).

The Christian obeys Christ when he searches the scriptures to find the kind of qualities which should mark his life and when, by a conscious effort, he tries to live in this way. He is adding to his faith. He is developing his character. He is working out the salvation, which God has worked into him.

There are no short cuts in this process. There is no "instant" Christianity. Living the Christian life involves personal zeal and effort. It includes a "right use of the means of grace", above all, of prayer and the Word. It means applying the lessons of the Word systematically to daily living. This takes time, effort, concentration, perseverance and sacrifice. But it produces fruit in a changed character, a transformed life-style and in the peaceable fruit of assurance of salvation. Christians obey Christ by remaining in him, by dying and rising with him and by seeing Christ reborn within them. They accomplish this through the Word and prayer. It produces growth, godly character and assurance of salvation.

HOME

Christ's kingdom affects home life. This is often a difficult sphere of witness for the Christian. Home is where people know us as we really are, our strengths and weaknesses. Home can be the acid test of our Christianity. Yet the Bible stresses the importance of living for Christ in the home. The Bible presents home life in terms of amazing potential, as a sphere for Christian living and witness.

Christian Life

Jesus has some important things to say about home and family. He teaches the sanctity of marriage and the limited conditions for divorce. He admires the rich ruler for honouring his parents as part of his careful observance of the commandments. He shows love and openness to children, demands that they should be cared for and rebukes those who lead them astray. On this background, Jesus requires allegiance to himself even over and above natural and rightful family ties.

> *""If anyone comes to me and does not hate his own father and mother and wife and children and brothers and sisters, yes, and even his own life, he cannot be my disciple"* (Luke 14:26).

The apostles, in their letters, pursue the importance of home-life and give precise instruction on particular aspects.

COURTSHIP

Christians are to marry "in the Lord", that is, Christians are only to marry those who are Christians. God's people in the Old Testament were commanded to marry those of the covenant race, a natural restriction. God's people in the New Testament must marry within the covenant people, a spiritual restriction. Paul explains that the Christian widow is

> *"free to marry anyone she wishes, but he must belong to the Lord"* (I Corinthians 7:39). (NIV)

Paul also advises the Corinthian Christians,

> *"Do not be yoked together with unbelievers"*
> (II Corinthians 6:14). (NIV)

This means that Christian young people must consciously seek out a Christian boyfriend or girlfriend in courtship days. They must refuse courtship with those who are not Christians. It is important to approach the matter at the very outset with this biblical teaching in mind. Otherwise, friendships begin, feelings grow and a break becomes much more difficult later. Eventually, young folk come seeking marriage and put their minister in an impossible situation, leaving him no option but to refuse marriage because it is contrary to God's Word.

For this reason, Christian young people should seek such friendship primarily within the church. This is not an unnatural restriction but a helpful guideline. After all, if they really love Christ they will want to obey his Word and have as a partner in life one who also loves Christ.

> *"For what do righteousness and wickedness have in common? Or what fellowship can light have with darkness . . . What does a believer have in common with an unbeliever?"* (II Corinthians 6:14, 15). (NIV)

MARRIAGE

The Apostolic writers regard marriage as a lifelong relationship characterised by love and faithfulness. Paul uses the picture of Christ as bridegroom and the church as bride to drive home this lesson. As Christ loved the church and gave himself for it, so husbands ought to love their wives. As the church submits gladly to Christ's love, so wives are to submit, not in a servile way, but happily to their husband's love and tender care

> *"Wives, submit to your husbands as to the Lord"*
>
> *"Husbands, love your wives, as Christ loved the church and gave himself up for her . . ."*
> (Ephesians 5:22, 25).

Peter writes of a submissive respect, which wives should have for their husbands, and of a considerate respect, which husbands should show to their wives

> *". . . wives, be subject to your own husbands, so that even if some do not obey the word, they may be won without a word by the conduct of their wives . . ."*
>
> *"Likewise, husbands, live with your wives in an understanding way, showing honour to the woman as the weaker vessel, since they are heirs with you of the grace of life, so that your prayers may not be hindered"* (I Peter 3:1, 7).

Christian Life

The writer to the Hebrews describes marriage as worthy of everyone's honour

> *"Let marriage be held in honour among all, and let the marriage bed be undefiled, for God will judge the sexually immoral and adulterous"* (Hebrews 13:4).

Christians within marriage ought to behave in accordance with this teaching. Husbands ought to be kind, considerate, tender and practically caring towards their wives. Wives ought to be happily submissive to such care and respond to it with a similar affection and practical love. Sexual relations must be reserved for marriage, neither before it nor outside it. Within marriage, this aspect deserves tenderness, consideration, self-control and unselfishness.

The New Testament also stresses the *"sanctifying"* nature of Christian marriage, that is, one partner helps the other in Christian growth. In a marriage, where one partner becomes a Christian, Paul describes the unbelieving partner as *"sanctified"* through the believing partner and the children as *"holy"* (I Corinthians 7:14). Peter urges wives to win their unbelieving husbands to faith *"without words"* through their Christian behaviour (I Peter 3:1).

This is exciting. It means that God's Word encourages Christian wives and husbands married to those who are not Christians to pray for their partner's conversion and to live in such a way at home that their partner will come to faith through the witness of their Christian living. Home is the first mission-field in the Christian's life. As husband, wife, father, mother or child the Christian is to win his family for Christ through prayer and a life-style in accordance with God's Word.

PARENTS

Paul gives helpful directions to Christian parents in the home.

> *"Fathers, do not provoke your children to anger, but bring them up in the discipline and instruction of the Lord."* (Ephesians 6:4).

Duties are spelled out clearly, for, while both parents are involved, fathers are particularly mentioned as primarily responsible. Negative warning is underlined, for parents can be overbearing in authority and can wrongly provoke children. Positive instruction is encouraged, for the words "training" and "instruction" speak of firm discipline and Paul uses the word "training" elsewhere to describe the usefulness of scripture

> *"All Scripture is breathed out by God and profitable for teaching, for reproof, for correction, and for training in righteousness . . ."* (II Timothy 3:16).

All of this means that Christian fathers must take the initiative and time for covenantal rearing and ought not to leave this responsibility to mothers or Sunday School teachers. Christian parents must guard against the pitfalls of unreasonable authoritarianism. On the other hand, clear firm lines of moral and spiritual instruction must be given and meaningfully implemented. The best way, of course, is, as Paul implies, through the training and instruction of scripture. "Family worship" can be a worthwhile development here. A short time, perhaps after evening meal, when the family listen to the Word and pray together in an informal setting, is an excellent practical application of Paul's directions. It can be made appropriate to the age-grouping. Discipline and training becomes warm and meaningful only when related to God's Word.

CHILDREN

Paul's instruction to children within the Christian home is equally helpful.

> *"Children, obey your parents in the Lord, for this is right. 'Honour your father and mother' (this is the first commandment with a promise), 'that it may go well with you and that you may live long in the land'"* (Ephesians 6:1-3).

Christian Life

The authority of the fifth commandment is regarded as binding and its covenantal nature is stressed. In the sometimes difficult years of adolescence, particularly, it helps young people to realise that, while they might regard their own judgment as correct, God still advises respect and obedience to parental authority. The guidelines are perpetual and the results remain the same.

Again the question arises - how can we live as Christians within the home? What can help us implement this teaching? The key to a developing Christian home and family life is facing up to covenant responsibilities. The covenant of grace brings the blessing of salvation to the believer and to his children. Salvation enters the home and, in God's purpose, spreads. But privilege involves responsibility. It is as we face up to our covenant duties, as Christian children and young people, husbands and wives, fathers and mothers through the Word, prayer and Christian living, that we rightly expect and enjoy God's blessing in the home.

CHURCH

Christ's kingdom is naturally evident in church life. We have already considered the church as a "means of grace" for the Christian. Here we think about this in the on-going sequence of the Christian life. The New Testament stresses three important aspects of the Christian's involvement in church life. Faithfulness, service and fellowship.

FAITHFULNESS

New communicants promise faithfulness to the church on reception into membership. Sometimes the words "diligent" and "duty" are involved. Often the vow includes the question, "Do you promise to make diligent use of the means of grace?" This is perfectly scriptural. Luke describes the on-going behaviour of those who had repented, been baptised and were added to the church on the day of Pentecost like this.

> *"And they devoted themselves to the apostles' teaching and the fellowship, to the breaking of bread and the prayers"* (Acts 2:42).

They made diligent use of the means of grace.

These were meaningful and important activities and, because of this, they required commitment. There was nothing haphazard or half-hearted about the involvement of the first Christians in these activities. These activities and the attitudes of the Christians to them were "marks" or characteristics of the early church. The church was recognisable by these things.

Christians today must be devoted to instruction, fellowship, the breaking of bread and prayer. As they gather together as a church, devotion to these things must be evident. Individually, Christians devote themselves to the Word and prayer at home. Corporately, also, their zeal for the Word and prayer and for fellowship and the breaking of bread is to be expected.

Devotion to these things or the lack of it affects the "credibility" of their profession both individually and corporately. If there is no desire for these things, we rightly doubt the reality of saving faith. It is not a matter of outer religious observance but of the living out of a personal faith.

This faithfulness, however, requires not only inner motivation but also practical commitment. Both concentration and consistency are involved. The writer to the Hebrews is quite explicit about this.

> *"And let us consider how to stir up one another to love and good works, not neglecting to meet together, as is the habit of some, but encouraging one another, and all the more as you see the Day drawing near"* (Hebrews 10:24,25).

We rightly expect to see Christians at both services on the Lord's Day, at Mid-week Fellowship and prayer meetings except, of course, when they have reason for absence, which they can conscientiously give to their Lord and Master Christ. This is the least they can offer in terms of faithfulness to a Lord who was faithful to death for them. Their presence shows their faithfulness. Their absence calls into question the credibility of their profession. The requirement is a demand of God's Word.

SERVICE

New communicants frequently promise *"to share dutifully in the worship and service of the Church"*. This conjures up pictures of singing lustily at worship, praying meaningfully along with the minister and listening attentively to the preaching of God's Word. Service involves this but it means much more.

The New Testament has many important things to say about service in the church. Peter describes Christians as living stones comprising God's temple, in which are offered spiritual sacrifices. Paul sees Christians as limbs in the body of Christ varying in function but all working together for the common good of the body. Jesus teaches that we should eagerly use our gifts and not bury them. Paul writes of the ascended Christ giving gifts to his church: apostles, prophets, evangelists, pastors and teachers,

> *"to equip the saints for the work of ministry, for building up the body of Christ"* (Ephesians 4:11, 12).

Paul also writes to Christians at Rome and Corinth about using their gifts. Some of these gifts are obviously "extraordinary" like miracles, speaking in tongues and prophecy. But, what does all this teach us about service?

First, it teaches that Christians are given gifts for service by the ascended Christ. We cannot claim inability for service because we have no gifts. Even if it is only one "talent", we must use it, not bury it.

Secondly, it helps us to recognise that there are "natural" gifts, that is, abilities or skills which God gives us as creatures in ordinary or "common" grace, the ability to teach or to type, the gift of music or the ability to make friends and help people, for example. God in salvation often develops these natural abilities in the person who becomes a Christian and they are used in Christian service.

Thirdly, there are "spiritual gifts", sometimes called "charismatic" gifts because they are gifts of God's CHARIS or grace. People immediately think of the supernatural gifts such as miracles, speaking in tongues and prophecy, mentioned in Corinthians. A good case can be made out that these gifts were limited to the apostolic days and were given as early confirmation of the gospel. Aside from the function of elders in ruling and teaching and of deacons in serving, the New Testament mentions as gifts, Christians doing good, showing mercy, teaching, encouraging, serving and giving to others. Let us develop gifts, which God has given to us, perhaps initially in "common" grace, and use them in service to God's glory in "special" grace. Particular mention ought to be made of giving as a form of service. Of course, we are urged to give ourselves as "living sacrifices" to God and this includes everything we are and have. But the New Testament stresses giving in terms of contributing money to God's work. This is why on most of our Freewill Weekly Offering envelopes we find the words

> *"On the first day of every week, each of you is to put something aside and store it up, as he may prosper, so that there will be no collecting when I come."*
> (I Corinthians 16:2).

A good guideline here is the practice of "tithing" or giving one tenth of our income to the Lord's work. This was the Old Testament practice of God's people. Jesus, in his teaching, implies confirmation of it. Certainly, the lavish nature of the giving of the New Testament church points in this direction. In determining the outlay of our tithe or tenth, it is important to assess realistically the needs of our own fellowship. Other worthy Christian and missionary causes should also be supported. Only then will we be fulfilling our vow.

Christian Life

FELLOWSHIP

Part of the "diligent use of the means of grace", which new communicants promise, is fellowship. Fellowship, as we have noted earlier, is more than friendship. It is Christians sharing together what they have in common, spiritually and practically.

Submission is one way the New Testament suggests of fostering fellowship. There must be submission in the Lord to our spiritual leaders, teaching and ruling elders, as they care for our souls and instruct us in the Word of God. We must heed their instruction and learn from it. There must also be mutual submission, for the apostolic teaching also requires this.

> *"submitting to one another out of reverence for Christ"* (Ephesians 5:21).

As we do this, regarding others as greater than ourselves and showing no favouritism, our fellowship deepens.

Sharing is another way of developing fellowship. The first Christians literally shared their possessions and goods with each other. They shared their problems, bearing one another's burdens thus fulfilling the law of Christ. They shared praise, encouraging one another in psalms, hymns and spiritual songs. They shared prayer, remembering one another before God. As we give, listen, weep, rejoice and pray altogether, we grow together.

How does our church life grow? What key factor holds together our faithfulness, service and fellowship? The answer here is relationships. As we work at cultivating our relationships within the church, Christ's kingdom expands and extends. Our faithfulness strengthens, our service develops and our fellowship deepens.

WORLD

Christ's kingdom must penetrate the world. The "world" in the sense of non-Christian society is described in the New Testament as alien to God. James writes,

> *"You adulterous people! Do you not know that friendship with the world is enmity with God? Therefore whoever wishes to be a friend of the world makes himself an enemy of God"* (James 4:4).

Christians need constantly to remember this. The friends we have, the places to which we go, the entertainment we enjoy, the attitude to current modes of life-style we adopt, the dangers of materialism must all be reviewed in the light of this principle. Christ prays not that we should be taken out of the world but rather preserved within the world. Christians are different people with totally different aims and objectives from those who are non-Christians. The world is alien not neutral to Christianity. Christians are not meant to imitate the world but to win the world for Christ. We do this, however, not by opting out but by remaining within the world's society. We are in the world but not of the world.

The New Testament suggests two areas particularly where the Christian can take the battle of Christ's kingdom to the world.

WORK

The way in which the Christian does his daily work is vitally important. However mundane and tiresome it may be, the New Testament regards daily work as a sphere of Christian service for Christ. In this sense, the distinction between "secular" and "sacred" does not apply. Everything our hands find to do, we are to do it with all our might. Whether we sweep streets or are a consultant surgeon, as Christians, we must all serve our master Christ. He is our master and to him, in the quality of our daily work, we are ultimately answerable.

This helps our purpose in the world. Of course, sweeping the street will just be as tiresome and back-breaking as ever and being a consultant surgeon as responsible and gratifying as before, but our attitude to the task is different. We approach our work, carry out our duties and bring the day's finished task to Christ for his approval to gladly hear his, "Well done". It also

Christian Life

helps our witness to the world. As society sees Christians carry out their daily work faithfully, efficiently and to the best of their ability, it concludes that Christianity really works.

The attitude of the Christian to daily work and work relationships is also significant. One of the most surprising things about New Testament teaching is that it never condemns the institution of slavery, yet, ultimately, slavery was abolished on the basis of Christian convictions. Indeed, both Paul and Peter advise slaves to obey their masters, even those who are harsh and inconsiderate. Christian masters are to treat their slaves with respect and sincerity. For in all, the principle of Christ as Lord, both of slave and master, is fundamental. Implementation of this principle promotes both the quality of work and working relationships.

This does not mean that cringing Christians are to be the order of the day at work. Nor does it imply that trade union activity is essentially non-Christian. What it means is that, whether Christians are at managerial or work-floor level, respect, justice, dignity, consideration and subjection to Christ's lordship should control activities and relationships. This again stimulates Christian purpose and enhances Christian witness.

CITIZENSHIP

The Christian's attitude to citizenship is the other sphere where he can take the battle for Christ's kingdom to the world. Christians are enjoined to be good citizens. As far as is possible, they are to live peaceably with all men. They are to pay their debts. They are to get on with their daily work in a quiet and efficient manner.

Their attitude to the authorities is particularly stressed. Both Paul and Peter require Christians to submit to the governing authorities on the grounds that those authorities are appointed by God for government. The purpose of that government is not only administrative but moral. The function of government is both to order society in a responsible fashion as well as to punish those who do wrong and commend those who do right. Thus, Christians are to pay taxes and revenue. They are to respect and obey those who govern them.

This does not mean that Christians remain totally passive. Christians have the responsibility of criticising government, where they regard it deficient in its God-given functions. They have also the responsibility of commending governments' implementation of its God-given task. This means, for example, campaigning against improper media productions, the extension of harmful social habits, stringent legal measures or punishments and the unbridled exhibition and advocacy of evil. It also means commending reform or improvement which has taken place. All legal methods of such criticism or commendation ought to be used. Resort to civil disobedience must only take place where the Christian is required to obey man rather than God. A more positive attitude would be Christians becoming involved in public life.

How can we effectively take the battle of the kingdom to the world? How can we live at daily work and under government that Christ's kingdom will penetrate the world? The answer is through Christian witness and, here, Jesus' teaching is most helpful.

Witness is through Christian proclamation. We must go into all the world, and that includes society on our own doorstep, and make disciples of all nations by teaching them to obey Christ's commands. We must do this uncompromisingly, realising that the world is alien to God and does not want to hear the gospel of Christ. But, as we persist in this proclamation, Christ's kingdom penetrates the world.

Witness is through Christian living. Jesus teaches that Christians are the salt of the earth and the light of the world. As salt, their witness is inner. As Christians live for Christ at work and under government, they preserve society from decay and deterioration. As light, their witness is outward. Society sees the quality of Christians' work, the integrity of their behaviour, their

Christian Life

thoughtfulness and consideration in relationships, their zeal for right, in a word, their "good deeds" and society praises God, the Father in heaven. Christian living aids the extension of Christ's kingdom in the world.

True communicant membership means not only becoming a Christian but also being a Christian. It involves living for Christ each day of our lives personally, at home, within church and in the world. As we develop our Christian obedience, responsibilities, relationships and witness in these spheres, we grow in grace and in the knowledge of Christ our Saviour to the glory of God our Father through the power of the Holy Spirit.

SUMMARY

Christian Life

PERSONAL LIFE

1. Who is the vine? (John 15:1-8)

   _____
   _____

2. Who is the Gardener - the one in control?

   _____
   _____

3. Who are the branches?

   _____
   _____

4. What does God do with the branches that bear fruit?

   _____
   _____

5. Can you think of practical examples as to how God might "prune us?

   _____
   _____
   _____
   _____
   _____

Christian Life

HOME LIFE

1. What is the most important principle for a Christian seeking a marriage partner?

   _____

   _____

   _____

   _____

2. From I Peter 3:1-7 list the responsibilities of husband and wives.

Husbands	Wives

3. From Ephesians 6:1-4, II Timothy 1:5 and II Timothy 3:14, 15 list the responsibilities of Christian parents and their children.

   _____

   _____

   _____

   _____

   _____

   _____

CHURCH LIFE

1. What degree of faithfulness should be expected from Christians to the Church. *See Acts 2:42 and Hebrews 10:25.*

   _____
   _____
   _____
   _____

2. Suggest what may be involved in serving the Church?

   _____
   _____
   _____
   _____

3. What is Christian fellowship and how should we develop it?

   _____
   _____
   _____
   _____

LIFE IN THE WORLD

1. What should the Christian attitude to the world be?
   See John 17:14-16 and James 4:4.

   _____
   _____
   _____
   _____

Christian Life

2. Colossians 3:22– 4:1 describes the Christian attitude for slaves and masters. These principles are still relevant today for employees and employers. From this passage suggest what "higher" motives should control the Christian at work.

   _____
   _____
   _____
   _____
   _____
   _____

3. From Romans 13:1-7 outline the Christians responsibility to the government of the country.

   _____
   _____
   _____
   _____
   _____

CHAPTER 8

THE HOLY SPIRIT

While the person and work of God the Father and God the Son are known and generally recognised, the person and work of God the Holy Spirit remains a mystery to many. The very name poses a problem. God the "Holy Spirit" or "Holy Ghost" conjures up pictures of some vague influence emanating from God; a force or power but certainly not a person, much less a divine person of the Triune Godhead.

PERSON

Yet that is not the biblical picture of the Holy Spirit. Even in the Old Testament the "Spirit of God" is much more than that. The force ordering the creation, inspiring the prophets, directing the mighty men and influencing nations is seen as much more than some dynamic atmosphere. Rather, it is the person of God at work among men.

Jesus, above all, puts the record straight about the person of the Holy Spirit (John 14:16, 19). Clearly, Jesus speaks of the Holy Spirit as a person here. The Holy Spirit is "another" counsellor, who continues Jesus' work in His absence. The Holy Spirit is described as "Him" not "It", to be seen, known and lived with, just as the disciples have seen, known and lived with Jesus, though obviously this person will be "invisible" to the human eye. Nevertheless, He will care for disciples just as Jesus had done so that they will not be left like orphans in Jesus' personal absence.

> *"And I will ask the Father, and he will give you another Helper, to be with you forever, even the Spirit of truth, whom the world cannot receive, because it neither sees him nor knows him. You know him, for he dwells with you and will be in you."*
> (John 14:16, 17).

What Presbyterians Believe

The rest of the New Testament bears out Jesus' description of the Holy Spirit as a person: the Spirit –

- **speaks,**

    "... *and said, 'Brothers, the Scripture had to be fulfilled, which the Holy Spirit spoke beforehand by the mouth of David concerning Judas, who became a guide to those who arrested Jesus...'"*
    (Acts 1:15, 16; Acts 8:29; 10:19; 11:12; 13:2; 28:25).

- **teaches,**

    "But the Helper, the Holy Spirit, whom the Father will send in my name, he will teach you all things and bring to your remembrance all that I have said to you" (John 14:26).

- **witnesses,**

    "'But when the Helper comes, whom I will send to you from the Father, the Spirit of truth, who proceeds from the Father, he will bear witness about me...'" (John 15:26).

- **searches,**

    "... *the Spirit searches everything, even the depths of God. For who knows a person's thoughts except the spirit of that person, which is in him? So also no one comprehends the thoughts of God except the Spirit of God"* (I Corinthians 2:10, 11).

- **determines,**

    "All these are empowered by one and the same Spirit, who apportions to each one individually as he wills" (I Corinthians 12:11).

- **intercedes,**

    "Likewise the Spirit helps us in our weakness. For we do not know what to pray for as we ought, but the Spirit himself intercedes for us with groanings too deep for words" (Romans 8:26).

The Holy Spirit

- **is lied to**,

    "But Peter said, 'Ananias, why has Satan filled your heart to lie to the Holy Spirit and to keep back for yourself part of the proceeds of the land?'" (Acts 5:3)

- **can be grieved**,

    "And do not grieve the Holy Spirit of God, by whom you were sealed for the day of redemption" (Ephesians 4:30).

These are all characteristics of a person not a thing.

The implication goes even further than personhood. Scripture makes clear that the Holy Spirit is a divine person, a person within the triune Godhead. The Holy Spirit is spoken of as on a par with the Father and Son, as seen in the benedictions[3] and in the commission to baptise.[4]

To lie to the Spirit is tantamount to lying to God

"But Peter said, 'Ananias, why has Satan filled your heart to lie to the Holy Spirit and to keep back for yourself part of the proceeds of the land? While it remained unsold, did it not remain your own? And after it was sold, was it not at your disposal? Why is it that you have contrived this deed in your heart? You have not lied to men but to God'" (Acts 5:3, 4).

Paul writes to Corinthian Christians of the Lord who is the Spirit as revealing Christ to believers and transforming their lives into the likeness of Christ.

"But when one turns to the Lord, the veil is removed.

---

[3] *"The grace of the Lord Jesus Christ and the love of God and the fellowship of the Holy Spirit be with you all"* (II Corinthians 13:14),

[4] *"Go therefore and make disciples of all nations, baptizing them in the name of the Father and of the Son and of the Holy Spirit,"* (Matthew 28:19).

133

> *Now the Lord is the Spirit, and where the Spirit of the Lord is, there is freedom. And we all, with unveiled face, beholding the glory of the Lord, are being transformed into the same image from one degree of glory to another. For this comes from the Lord who is the Spirit"* (II Corinthians 3:16, 17, 18).

John sees in his vision on Patmos the Spirit as "Seven Spirits" – seven being the number signifying divine perfection,

> *"John to the seven churches that are in Asia:*
>
> *Grace to you and peace from him who is and who was and who is to come, and from the seven spirits who are before his throne, ..."* (Revelation 1:4).
>
> *"From the throne came flashes of lightning, and rumblings and peals of thunder, and before the throne were burning seven torches of fire, which are the seven spirits of God"* (Revelation 4:5).
>
> *"And between the throne and the four living creatures and among the elders I saw a Lamb standing, as though it had been slain, with seven horns and with seven eyes, which are the seven spirits of God sent out into all the earth"* (Revelation 5:6).

The exciting thing about all this for Christians is that God's person and presence is with us day by day in the Holy Spirit. He is God the Spirit relating to us. Jesus' description of the Holy Spirit as the Counsellor carries with it all the expertise of one who comes to give us advice, and all the warm intimacy of a friend who does this personally so that we do not feel orphaned. What a real friend the Holy Spirit is.

> "In the unity of the Godhead there are three persons, of one substance, power and eternity: God the Father, God the Son, and God the Holy Spirit. The order seen in the external operations of the three persons reflects the eternal reality that each person possesses a property distinct from the others: the Father eternally possesses fatherhood in relation to the Son, the Son is eternally the son

The Holy Spirit

> *of the Father and the Spirit is eternally from the Father and the Son"* (W.C. 2:3).

WORK

The work of the Holy Spirit is equally impressive. God the Spirit works both in **common grace**, that is, the affairs of daily life of all creation, and in **special grace**, that is, the spiritual dimension of re-creation, where man is brought into a personal saving relationship with God. The intriguing thing about both these areas of the Spirit's work is the similarity. God's Spirit carries into practical effect the plan of God the Father and the provision of God the Son both in common and special grace. This work of "application" has about it a confirming and authenticating note in both spheres. The Spirit of God assures of the grace of the covenant God in creation, revelation and redemption.

CREATION

The Holy Spirit's work in creation is seen in a continuing work of providence for that creation. The Spirit's involvement in creation is stated right at the outset of Scripture

> *"In the beginning, God created the heavens and the earth. The earth was without form and void, and darkness was over the face of the deep. And the Spirit of God was hovering over the face of the waters"* (Genesis 1:1, 2).

The psalmist recalls this also in his song of creation

> *"By the word of the Lord the heavens were made, and by the breath of his mouth all their host"* (Psalm 33:6).

This picture of God's Spirit becomes even more vivid as we remember the Hebrew word for "spirit," means a strong, sharp breath or wind. God breathed into man's nostrils the breath of life and he became a living being is the unique way man's creation is depicted.

> *"then the Lord God formed the man of dust from the ground and breathed into his nostrils the breath of life, and the man became a living creature"* (Genesis 2:7).

But the Spirit of God, having initiated the creation, did not leave it or abandon it. He continues to supervise that creation which he has brought into being. So, the Spirit of God strives with man but not forever

> *"Then the Lord said, 'My Spirit shall not abide in man forever, for he is flesh: his days shall be 120 years'"* (Genesis 6:3).

and

> *". . . they rebelled and grieved his Holy Spirit; therefore he turned to be their enemy, and himself fought against them"* (Isaiah 63:10).

God cares lovingly for his creation

> *"The Lord is good to all, and his mercy is over all that he has made"* (Psalm 145:9; Psalm 145:15, 16; Acts 14).

God gives man a certain ability to do good

> *"And the Lord said to Jehu, 'Because you have done well in carrying out what is right in my eyes, and have done to the house of Ahab according to all that was in my heart, your sons of the fourth generation shall sit on the throne of Israel'"* (II Kings 10:30),

> *"And if you do good to those who do good to you, what benefit is that to you? For even sinners do the same"* (Luke 6: 33; Romans 2: 14-15).

He restrains evil[5] and delays punishment in order to offer opportunity for repentance and faith

---

[5] *". . . yet your father has cheated me and changed my wages ten times. But God did not permit him to harm me"* (Genesis 31:7; Job 1:12; 2:6).

The Holy Spirit

> "*Or do you presume on the riches of his kindness and forbearance and patience, not knowing that God's kindness is meant to lead you to repentance?*"
> (Romans 2: 4; II Peter 3:9).

What a blessing to live in an ordered and not a chaotic universe, to have food to eat, clothes to wear, health to enjoy and purposeful work to do. These are the benefits given by God's Spirit to us in common grace. Whatever exceptions occur to these general rules: the righteous contracting terminal cancer, the evil enjoying health and wealth, we do not live in an amoral world. Even our own total depravity is restrained by God's Spirit, so that we are not as evil as we might be. We note these benefits in God's covenant with Noah following the judgement of the creation (Genesis 8:20-9:17). The work of God's Spirit in creation continues in His work of providence.

> "*The work of creation is the work God did in the beginning by his powerful word and for himself, when he made of nothing the world and all things in it, within the space of six days, and all very good*" (L.C. 15).

> "*The providence of God toward man in the state in which he was created was placing him in paradise, appointing him to work it and giving him liberty to eat of the produce of the earth; putting the creatures under his rule and ordaining marriage for his help; granting him communion with himself; instituting the Sabbath; entering into a covenant of life with him on condition of personal, perfect and perpetual obedience, of which the tree of life was a pledge; and forbidding him to eat of the tree of the knowledge of good and evil on penalty of death*" (L.C. 20).

REVELATION

The Holy Spirit's work in revelation is confirmed in signs following that revelation. The Spirit of God reveals God's word through the prophets in the Old Testament. Isaiah is conscious of the Spirit of the Sovereign Lord being upon him, as he preaches good news to the poor

> *"The Spirit of the Lord God is upon me . . ."*
> (Isaiah 61:1).

Micah, compared with false leaders and false prophets, is aware of being filled with the Spirit of the Lord as he declared to Israel his sin

> *"But as for me, I am filled with power, with the Spirit of the Lord, and with justice and might, to declare to Jacob his transgression and to Israel his sin"*
> (Micah 3:8).

Ezekiel, in the valley of dry bones, hears those bones rattling, as he proclaims the word of the Lord. But it is only as the Spirit breathes from the four winds that the dead flesh and bones stand on their feet and became a vast and living army of God,

> *"The hand of the Lord was upon me, and he brought me out in the Spirit of the Lord and set me down in the middle of the valley; it was full of bones"*
> (Ezekial 37:1f.).

Again, it is Jesus who specifies clearly the Spirit's work of revelation

> *"These things I have spoken to you while I am still with you. But the Helper, the Holy Spirit, whom the Father will send in my name, he will teach you all things and bring to your remembrance all that I have said to you. Peace I leave with you; my peace I give to you. Not as the world gives do I give to you. Let not your hearts be troubled, neither let them be afraid"* (John 14:25, 26, 27).

and

> *"'I still have many things to say to you, but you cannot bear them now. When the Spirit of truth comes, he will guide you into all the truth, for he will not speak on his own authority, but whatever he hears he will speak, and he will declare to you the things that are to come. He will glorify me, for he*

The Holy Spirit

> *will take what is mine and declare it to you . . .'"*
> (John 16:12, 13, 14).

Jesus calls the Holy Spirit "The Spirit of truth". This is a remarkable description. It means that, just as Jesus' teaching is absolute and precise truth and so the answer to all our needs, so the Spirit instructs us in Christ's teaching and points to Christ as the solution of all our problems. It means, too, that just as Jesus himself claimed to be genuine and real truth, so the Holy Spirit talks of Christ and makes him known to us. The Spirit's work is recalling the past and revealing the future. The Holy Spirit is like a flashing neon sign pointing not to itself but to the commodity advertised, highlighting the commodity's importance alone, a constant, continuing reminder which needs to be taken seriously.

The rest of the New Testament bears out this work of the Spirit and shows it confirmed with subsequent signs. Peter traces the origin of revelation to the Holy Spirit

> *"For no prophecy was ever produced by the will of man, but men spoke from God as they were carried along by the Holy Spirit"* (II Peter 1: 21).

Paul attributes the function of revelation to the Holy Spirit

> *"And we impart this in words not taught by human wisdom but taught by the Spirit, interpreting spiritual truths to those who are spiritual.*
>
> *The natural person does not accept the things of the Spirit of God, for they are folly to him, and he is not able to understand them because they are spiritually discerned. The spiritual person judges all things, but is himself to be judged by no one"*
> (I Corinthians 2:13-15).

It is in this context that the gifts of the Holy Spirit are to be seen in the New Testament. They are signs confirming the revelation of Jesus Christ by the Holy Spirit. Mark speaks of the disciples preaching everywhere and the Lord confirming his word with signs accompanying it.

> *"And they went out and preached everywhere, while the Lord worked with them and confirmed the message by accompanying signs"* (Mark 16:20).

Paul writes to Galatian Christians of the Spirit working miracles among them because they believed what they heard

> *"Does he who supplies the Spirit to you and works miracles among you do so by works of the law, or by hearing with faith?"* (Galatians 3:5).

The writer to the Hebrews describes salvation as first announced by the Lord, confirmed by those who heard him and authenticated by signs, wonders and various miracles, and gifts of the Holy Spirit distributed according to his will

> *". . . how shall we escape if we neglect such a great salvation? It was declared at first by the Lord, and it was attested to us by those who heard, while God also bore witness by signs and wonders and various miracles and by gifts of the Holy Spirit distributed according to his will"* (Hebrews 2:3, 4).

Luke in Acts not only describes the coming of the Spirit with accompanying signs on the day of Pentecost, but successively discloses how those miraculous signs attested the gospel and the coming of the Spirit, as the gospel message spread to Samaritans, Gentiles and also to incompletely instructed disciples at Ephesus (Acts 2:14; 8:4-25; 10:44-48; and 19:1-7). This was exactly as Jesus foretold

> *"'But you will receive power when the Holy Spirit has come upon you, and you will be my witnesses in Jerusalem and in all Judea and Samaria, and to the end of the earth'"* (Acts 1:8).

Luke is not suggesting that for each believer the Spirit comes at a time subsequent to conversion and that each believer attests this by "speaking in tongues". Rather, he is showing how the pattern previewed by Jesus concerning the Spirit's coming was confirmed by miraculous signs at each important stage of its extension (Acts 1:8). The **gifts** of the Spirit affirm the

proclamation of the gospel. The **fruit** of the Spirit attest the **experience** of the gospel.

> *"But the fruit of the Spirit is love, joy, peace, patience, kindness, goodness, faithfulness, gentleness, self-control . . ."* (Galatians 5:22-23).

Historically, Presbyterians would hold to the cessation of the miraculous gifts, as being confirming apostolic signs. These signs became unnecessary with the Spirit's written testimony in Scripture. The Spirit's revelation is completed in the written Word of God.

> *". . . Therefore it pleased the Lord at different times and in various ways to reveal himself, and to declare his will to his church. Afterwards, for the better preservation and propagation of the truth, and for the more sure establishment and comfort of the church against the corruption of the human heart, and the malice of Satan and of the world, God was pleased to commit this revelation of himself and his will wholly to written form. Accordingly, the Holy Scripture is now essential, for God's former ways of revealing his will to his people have ceased.*
>
> *Under the name of Holy Scripture, or the word of God written, are now comprised all the books of the Old and New Testaments, . . . all of these are given by inspiration of God to be the rule of faith and the life"* (W.C. 1:1, 2).
>
> *"The whole will of God concerning all things necessary for his own glory, and for our salvation, faith and life, is either expressly stated in Scripture, or by good and necessary reasoning may be deduced from Scripture. Nothing, whether new revelations of the Spirit or human tradition, is ever to be added to Scripture. Nevertheless, we acknowledge the inward illumination of the Spirit of God to be necessary for the saving understanding of the things that are revealed in the word. We also acknowledge that there are some circumstances concerning the worship of God and the government of the church, circumstances common to human actions and societies, which are*

> *to be arranged by natural intelligence and Christian prudence, but always in line with the general rules of God's word"* (W.C. 1:6).

REDEMPTION

The Holy Spirit's work of redemption is authenticated by his assuring salvation in the believer's life. In the Old Testament, the coming of the Spirit is predicted, not just for specific tasks but also for revealing salvation

> *"And it shall come to pass afterward, that I will pour out my Spirit on all flesh; your sons and your daughters shall prophesy, your old men shall dream dreams, and your young men shall see visions. Even on the male and female servants in those days I will pour out my Spirit.*
>
> *And I will show wonders in the heavens and on the earth, blood and fire and columns of smoke. The sun shall be turned to darkness, and the moon to blood, before the great and awesome day of the Lord comes. And it shall come to pass that everyone who calls on the name of the Lord shall be saved. For in Mount Zion and in Jerusalem there shall be those who escape, as the Lord has said, and among the survivors shall be those whom the Lord calls"* (Joel 2:28-32).
>
> *"For I will pour water on the thirsty land, and streams on the dry ground; I will pour my Spirit upon your offspring, and my blessing on your descendants. They shall spring up among the grass like willows by flowing streams. This one will say, 'I am the Lord's,' another will call on the name of Jacob, and another will write on his hand, 'The Lord's,' and name himself by the name of Israel"* (Isaiah 44:3, 4, 5).

So, eventually, John the Baptist promises that while he baptises with water, Jesus will baptise with the Holy Spirit.

> *"I baptize you with water for repentance, but he who is coming after me is mightier than I, whose*

The Holy Spirit

> *sandals I am not worthy to carry. He will baptize you with the Holy Spirit and fire"*
> (Matthew 3:11; Mark 1:8).

Jesus explains this work of the Holy Spirit in redemption in **two ways. The Spirit works sovereignly**

> *"The wind blows where it wishes, and you hear its sound, but you do not know where it comes from or where it goes. So it is with everyone who is born of the Spirit"* (John 3:8).

The Holy Spirit is likened to the wind. Just as we often cannot determine the wind's direction but can see its effect in fallen slates, broken branches and uprooted trees, so it is with the Spirit of God in redemption. He works sovereignly but effectively. **The Spirit also works savingly**

> *"Nevertheless, I tell you the truth: it is to your advantage that I go away, for if I do not go away, the Helper will not come to you. But if I go, I will send him to you. And when he comes, he will convict the world concerning sin and righteousness and judgment: concerning sin, because they do not believe in me; concerning righteousness, because I go to the Father, and you will see me no longer; concerning judgment, because the ruler of this world is judged"* (John 16:7-11).

The Holy Spirit is an advisor or legal counsellor. He persuades mankind that they are sinners. He acquits sinners of their sin through the righteousness of Christ and warns of the danger of imminent judgement. This advice is given because Jesus the Messiah has come and man either must accept or reject him as Saviour.

The Shorter Catechism sums up the Spirit's work in this way

> *"The Spirit applieth to us the redemption purchased by Christ, by working faith in us, and thereby uniting us to Christ in our effectual calling"*
> (S.C. 30).

© "Confession of Faith and Subordinate Standards" The Free Church of Scotland

Effectual calling, an old expression for regeneration, is

explained in these terms:

> *"Effectual calling is the work of God's Spirit, whereby, convincing us of our sin and misery, enlightening our minds in the knowledge of Christ, and renewing our wills, he doth persuade and enable us to embrace Jesus Christ, freely offered to us in the gospel"* (S.C. 31).

© "Confession of Faith and Subordinate Standards" The Free Church of Scotland

The rest of the New Testament underlines the Spirit's work of redemption especially as the Spirit authenticates salvation. Both Paul and Peter ascribe the Spirit's work in salvation within a triune setting: God the Father plans, God the son provides and God the Spirit, as it were, processes salvation.

> *". . . we have been chosen according to the foreknowledge of God the Father, by the sanctifying work of the Spirit, for obedience to Jesus Christ and sprinkling by his blood . . ."* (I Peter 1:2). (NIV)

In this way, the Holy Spirit carries into effect or applies salvation to mankind.

> *"In him you also, when you heard the word of truth, the gospel of your salvation, and believed in him, were sealed with the promised Holy Spirit, who is the guarantee of our inheritance until we acquire possession of it, to the praise of his glory"* (Ephesians 1:13, 14).

Paul uses two vivid metaphors to show the authenticating work of the Spirit in salvation. The Holy Spirit is **a seal** of salvation. The idea is of a seal confirming ownership. God possesses us in covenant by giving us the Holy Spirit in salvation, who witnesses with our spirit that we are God's children and enables us to cry, familiarly, "Abba" or "Daddy" to God in the intimacy of this new relationship. The Holy Spirit is also **a deposit** of salvation. This idea is of a down payment or a pledge promising future acquisition of something. In modern Greek, the word is used of an engagement ring. This perfectly describes the situation. God pledges His love to us in covenant by giving us the Holy Spirit in

The Holy Spirit

salvation, who begins the loving relationship with us which matures with Christ the Bridegroom: Our engagement is, thus, to be the Lord's.

One result of this authenticating work of the Holy Spirit is the growth of the fruit of the Spirit in our lives. As we "live by the Spirit," are "led by the Spirit," and "keep in step with the Spirit," the fruit of the Spirit appears in our lives (Galatians 5:16-26). The **gifts** of the Spirit confirm the revelation of the gospel. The **fruit** of the Spirit authenticates the redemption of the gospel.

> *"But I say, walk by the Spirit, and you will not gratify the desires of the flesh. For the desires of the flesh are against the Spirit, and the desires of the Spirit are against the flesh, for these are opposed to each other, to keep you from doing the things you want to do. But if you are led by the Spirit, you are not under the law. Now the works of the flesh are evident: sexual immorality, impurity, sensuality, idolatry, sorcery, enmity, strife, jealousy, fits of anger, rivalries, dissensions, divisions, envy, drunkenness, orgies, and things like these. I warn you, as I warned you before, that those who do such things will not inherit the kingdom of God. But the fruit of the Spirit is love, joy, peace, patience, kindness, goodness, faithfulness, gentleness, self-control; against such things there is no law. And those who belong to Christ Jesus have crucified the flesh with its passions and desires.*
>
> *If we live by the Spirit, let us also walk by the Spirit. Let us not become conceited, provoking one another, envying one another"* (Galatians 5:16-26).

How glorious is the work of God's Holy Spirit. He applies and assures the redemption purchased for us by Christ, imputing it to us in justification and infusing it in us in sanctification.

PERSEVERANCE OF THE SAINTS

> "This perseverance of the saints does not depend on their own free will, but on the unchangeable

decree of election flowing from the free and unchangeable love of God the Father; on the powerful operation of the merit and intercession of Jesus Christ; on the indwelling of the Spirit and of the life of God within them; and on the nature of the covenant of grace. These grounds provide the certainty and infallibility of the perseverance of the saints" (W.C. 17:2).

ASSURANCE OF GRACE AND SALVATION

"This certainty is not mere conjecture and probability based on a fallible hope, but is an infallible assurance arising from saving faith and based on the divine truth of the promises of salvation, the evidence in our hearts of those graces to which these promises are made, and the testimony of the Spirit of adoption witnessing with our spirits that we are the children of God. The Spirit is the pledge guaranteeing our inheritance, and by him we are sealed for the day of redemption" (W.C. 18:2).

The Holy Spirit

SUMMARY

Holy Spirit

PERSON AND WORK

1. In your own words, who is the Holy Spirit?

   _____
   _____
   _____
   _____

2. How does the Holy Spirit help us in the Christian life?

   _____
   _____
   _____
   _____

CREATION

3. List some of the benefits of God's Spirit in creation and providence.

   _____
   _____
   _____

REVELATION

4. What is the holy Spirit's role in divine revelation?

   _____
   _____
   _____

5. What is the purpose of the miraculous signs as described in Acts?

REDEMPTION

6. What does the picture of the Holy Spirit as "wind" or "breath" teach us about his work in redemption?

7. Conduct a spiritual health check, using the fruit of the Spirit as a list in Galatians 5:22-23.

NB *These are spiritual qualities, not the natural characteristics of someone with a pleasant disposition or nice personality*

Work through the list and ask yourself if this is evident, at least to some degree, in your life.

CHAPTER 9

THE LAST THINGS

The story of the Bible is not an unending cycle of events, which keeps going on forever and ever. It moves towards a climax. There is a finality about it. Two things, above all, mark the end of the story, one from the divine point of view, as it were, and one from the human. Both are inter-related. The divine is the Return or Second Coming of the Lord Jesus Christ. The human is the Judgement of mankind. In the Old Testament this was anticipated as the "Day of the Lord". In the New Testament it is featured as the "Last Day". In the new Testament also, the Greek words *parousia*, which describes the arrival of a royal presence, and *epiphancia*, which depicts the revealing or unveiling of something previously hidden, are used of Christ's return. Usually the New Testament words "last days" are used for the entire period from Jesus' first to his second coming and not just for the period immediately preceding his Return. We all move toward this event and we all face its implications.

THE SECOND COMING

The person of Christ lies at the very heart of this event. Scripture teaches that Jesus will come again. Jesus Himself makes this claim

> *"Then will appear in heaven the sign of the Son of Man, and then all the tribes of the earth will mourn, and they will see the Son of Man coming on the clouds of heaven with power and great glory"* (Matthew 24:30).

> *"In my Father's house are many rooms. If it were not so, would I have told you that I go to prepare a place for you? And if I go and prepare a place for you, I will come again and will take you to myself, that where I am you may be also"* (John 14:2, 3).

It will be a public return for He will return in body, similar to his ascension, and all eyes of all ages will see Him

> "... 'Men of Galilee, why do you stand looking into heaven? This Jesus, who was taken up from you into heaven, will come in the same way as you saw him go into heaven'" (Acts 1:11; Revelation 1:7).

It will be a disturbing occasion for it will be unexpected and will take people by surprise

> *For you yourselves are fully aware that the day of the Lord will come like a thief in the night"* (I Thessalonians 5:2; Matthew 24:37-44).

It will be a majestic event

> *"Then will appear in heaven the sign of the Son of Man, and then all the tribes of the earth will mourn, and they will see the Son of Man coming on the clouds of heaven with power and great glory"* (Matthew 24:30; II Thessalonians 1:7; I Thessalonians 3:13; II Thessalonians 1:10).

Above all, it will be a personal return. Jesus, who has come once as Saviour and Lord, will then return as Judge to bring all things to a close

> *"For the Lord himself will descend from heaven with a cry of command, with the voice of an archangel, and with the sound of the trumpet of God. And the dead in Christ will rise first"* (I Thessalonians 4:16).

God the Son will return, appointed by God the Father as Judge of all the living and the dead, to bring all things to completion.

> *"The Father judges no one, but has given all judgment to the Son, that all may honour the Son, just as they honour the Father. Whoever does not honour the Son does not honour the Father who sent him"* (John 5:22, 23).

The work of Christ is plainly evident in all this. It is a work

The Last Things

that involves separation. It marks the separation of mankind from one another. Christ in judgement will separate the wheat from the weeds and the sheep from the goats. He will consign them to their eternal destiny, either to heaven or to hell

> *"He put another parable before them, saying, 'The kingdom of heaven may be compared to a man who sowed good seed in his field, but while his men were sleeping, his enemy came and sowed weeds among the wheat and went away. So when the plants came up and bore grain, then the weeds appeared also.*
>
> *And the servants of the master of the house came and said to him, 'Master, did you not sow good seed in your field? How then does it have weeds?'*
>
> *He said to them, 'An enemy has done this.'*
>
> *So the servants said to him, 'Then do you want us to go and gather them?'*
>
> *But he said, 'No, lest in gathering the weeds you root up the wheat along with them'"* (Matthew 13:24-29).
>
> *"Then he left the crowds and went into the house. And his disciples came to him, saying, 'Explain to us the parable of the weeds of the field.' He answered, 'The one who sows the good seed is the Son of Man. The field is the world, and the good seed is the sons of the kingdom. The weeds are the sons of the evil one, and the enemy who sowed them is the devil. The harvest is the close of the age, and the reapers are angels. Just as the weeds are gathered and burned with fire, so will it be at the close of the age'"* (Matthew 13:36-40),

and

> *"When the Son of Man comes in his glory, and all the angels with him, then he will sit on his glorious throne. Before him will be gathered all the nations, and he will separate people one from another as a shepherd separates the sheep from the goats. And he*

151

> *will place the sheep on his right, but the goats on the left . . ."* (Matthew 25:31-43).

It involves the separation of mankind from God. On this same day of judgement, those who do not obey the gospel of Christ will be punished by being banished from God's presence

> *". . . and with all wicked deception for those who are perishing, because they refused to love the truth and so be saved"* (II Thessalonians 2:10).

This does not conflict with the doctrine of God's omnipresence, since unbelievers will be excluded from the loving presence of God but, at the same time, experience His wrathful judgement. Indeed, this work of judgement marks a separation in function of the "two" comings of Christ. On the first occasion, Christ was once sacrificed to take away the sins of many people. On the second, He appears not for the purpose of bearing sin but to bring salvation to those waiting for him and to punish the rest of mankind, since it is appointed to men to die once, after which comes judgement

> *"And just as it is appointed for man to die once, and after that comes judgment, so Christ, having been offered once to bear the sins of many, will appear a second time, not to deal with sin but to save those who are eagerly waiting for him"* (Hebrews 9:27, 28).

The entire purpose of Christ's work as Judge is to manifest God's glory and display his justice

> *"What if God, desiring to show his wrath and to make known his power, has endured with much patience vessels of wrath prepared for destruction, in order to make known the riches of his glory for vessels of mercy, which he has prepared beforehand for glory . . ."* (Romans 9:22, 23).

THE GATHERING OF GOD'S PEOPLE

If the work of Christ at His return involves separation for the unbeliever, gathering is the keynote of that event for the believer.

The Last Things

Jesus forecasts how the Son of Man *". . . will send out the angels and gather his elect from the four winds, from the ends of the earth to the ends of heaven"* (Mark 13:27). Paul assures the Thessalonian Church that Christians who have died before Christ's return will not be disadvantaged. They will rise first, be caught up with those who are still alive, meet the Lord in the air and so will be with the Lord for ever (I Thessalonians 4:16-17). Paul further describes that event in contrasting terms: those punished with everlasting destruction, shut out from the presence of the Lord; those for whom Christ will be glorified in His holy people and marvelled at among all who have believed

> *"They will suffer the punishment of eternal destruction, away from the presence of the Lord and from the glory of his might, when he comes on that day to be glorified in his saints, and to be marveled at among all who have believed, because our testimony to you was believed"*
> (II Thessalonians 1:9, 10).

What a wonderful gathering of togetherness and fellowship Christ's return will bring to believers!

THE SIGNS OF THE SECOND COMING

The time of the Second Coming has been a constant subject of discussion within the Christian Church. Often it has generated more heat than light. Scripture teaches that the time of this occurrence is hidden from man.

> *"But concerning that day and hour no one knows, not even the angels of heaven, nor the Son, but the Father only"* (Matthew 24:36).

> *"Therefore stay awake – for you do not know when the master of the house will come, in the evening, or at midnight, or when the rooster crows, or in the morning –"* (Mark 13:35).

Certain identifiable events, however, are noted in Scripture as occurring before Christ returns. These include:

153

The calling of the Gentiles
The gospel must be preached to all peoples before the return of Christ

> *"And this gospel of the kingdom will be proclaimed throughout the whole world as a testimony to all nations, and then the end will come"* (Matthew 24:14).
>
> *"And the gospel must first be proclaimed to all nations."* (Mark 13:10).
>
> *"Lest you be wise in your own sight, I want you to understand this mystery, brothers: a partial hardening has come upon Israel, until the fullness of the Gentiles has come in"* (Romans 11:25).

The conversion of Israel
Paul writing to both the Church at Corinth and at Rome suggests that Israel will be converted to Christ

> *"Yes, to this day whenever Moses is read a veil lies over their hearts. But when one turns to the Lord, the veil is removed"* (2 Corinthians 3:15,16; Romans 11:25-29).

Particularly in Romans this is linked with the Last Day. When Paul itemises **"all Israel"** he may well refer to the full number of the elect from God's ancient chosen people not the totality of the Israelite nation.

> *"And in this way **all Israel** will be saved, as it is written,*
> *'The Deliverer will come from Zion, he will banish ungodliness from Jacob'; 'and this will be my covenant with them when I take away their sins'"* (Romans 11:26-27).

THE GREAT APOSTASY AND THE GREAT TRIBULATION

While there are general references to these features, the New Testament does indicate a specific falling away and special time

The Last Things

of hardship. There will be an increase in godlessness and a coldness of love in many.[6] An awful tribulation never known before or thereafter will occur, shortened only for the sake of God's people.

> *"For then there will be great tribulation, such as has not been from the beginning of the world until now, no, and never will be"* (Matthew 24:21).

THE COMING OF ANTICHRIST

The spirit of Antichrist will be abroad in those days and antichrists will actually appear.

> *"Children, it is the last hour, and as you have heard that antichrist is coming, so now many antichrists have come. Therefore we know that it is the last hour"* (I John 2:18; I John 4:3).

However the Bible is quite specific as to a single individual; "the man of lawlessness" who "opposes and exalts himself over everything that is called God," and "even sets himself up in God's temple, proclaiming himself to be God"

> *"Let no one deceive you in any way. For that day will not come, unless the rebellion comes first, and the man of lawlessness is revealed, the son of destruction, who opposes and exalts himself against every so-called god or object of worship, so that he takes his seat in the temple of God, proclaiming himself to be God"* (II Thessalonians 2:3, 4).

SIGNS AND WONDERS

Striking portents, wars, famines, earthquakes, the birth pangs of the new universe, will occur,

---

[6] *"And because lawlessness will be increased, the love of many will grow cold"* (Matthew 24:12; II Thessalonians 2:3).

> *""Immediately after the tribulation of those days the sun will be darkened, and the moon will not give its light, and the stars will fall from heaven, and the powers of the heavens will be shaken. Then will appear in heaven the sign of the Son of Man, and then all the tribes of the earth will mourn, and they will see the Son of Man coming on the clouds of heaven with power and great glory"*
> (Matthew 24:29, 30).
>
> *"And there will be signs in sun and moon and stars, and on the earth distress of nations in perplexity because of the roaring of the sea and the waves, people fainting with fear and with foreboding of what is coming on the world. For the powers of the heavens will be shaken"*
> (Luke 21:25, 26; Mark 13:24, 25).

THE MILLENNIUM

Millennium, which means one thousand years, is used in Scripture to describe part of John's vision on Patmos (Revelation 20:1-6). There have been three interpretations of this Millennium. Arising from this and other biblical data about the return of Christ, certain views of the order of events have been suggested, especially in view of Christ's reign of one thousand years, the Millennium, mentioned in Revelation 20:1-6

> *"Then I saw an angel coming down from heaven, holding in his hand the key to the bottomless pit and a great chain. And he seized the dragon, that ancient serpent, who is the devil and Satan, and bound him for a thousand years, and threw him into the pit, and shut it and sealed it over him, so that he might not deceive the nations any longer, until the thousand years were ended. After that he must be released for a little while.*
>
> *Then I saw thrones, and seated on them were those to whom the authority to judge was committed. Also I saw the souls of those who had been beheaded for the testimony of Jesus and for the word of God, and*

The Last Things

> *those who had not worshipped the beast or its image and had not received its mark on their foreheads or their hands. They came to life and reigned with Christ for a thousand years. The rest of the dead did not come to life until the thousand years were ended. This is the first resurrection. Blessed and holy is the one who shares in the first resurrection! Over such the second death has no power, but they will be priests of God and of Christ, and they will reign with him for a thousand years."* (Revelation 20:1-6).

PREMILLENNIALISM

teaches that Christ will first return and then establish His kingdom on earth, where He will reign in Jerusalem for one thousand years. This, however, is based on a **literalistic interpretation** of Revelation 20:1-6, portrays Christ's kingdom as **earthly** rather than spiritual, requires, in effect, <u>"two" returns of Christ and "two" separate judgements</u>, projects a millennium where resurrected and unresurrected live side by side and implies the existence of evil after Christ's return. Many premillenialism's "unfulfilled" promises have, in fact, been fulfilled in Christ. All of this reasoning is contrary to the tenor of Scripture.

POSTMILLENNIALISM

claims that Christ will return after a millennial period marked by great success in gospel preaching and widespread growth in righteousness and spiritual blessing. One difficulty with this view is relating it to the disturbing events itemised in Scripture before Christ's return, such as, the Great Apostasy and Tribulation and the appearance of Antichrist. Another difficulty is that Scripture portrays the future not in terms of a growing "golden age" but of a continuing suffering church.

AMILLENNIALISM

literally 'without a millennium' holds that Revelation 20:1-6, being a **figurative description**, should be interpreted in the light of the other evidence concerning Christ's Return in the New Testament. On this understanding, there are insufficient grounds for the expectation of a millennium. Rather, the present dispensation of the kingdom of God will be followed immediately by the kingdom of God in its consummate form. The millennium of Revelation 20:1-6, from this viewpoint, is a figurative expression of Christ's rule between the two advents, Christ's coming and Christ's return.

The purpose of biblical teaching of Christ's return is not speculation but sanctification. Godly living rather than idle curiosity should be the result of contemplating the Second Coming. Service for Christ should also be a result. Jesus, in the parable, urges the servants to work hard until the king returned:

> "Calling ten of his servants, he gave them ten minas, and said to them, 'Engage in business until I come'" (Luke 19:13).

Paul recalls the importance of building a worthy superstructure on Christ the foundation. Otherwise, one would be saved, but with little to show for it, but only as one escaping through the flames

> "According to the grace of God given to me, like a skilled master builder I laid a foundation, and someone else is building upon it. Let each one take care how he builds upon it. For no one can lay a foundation other than that which is laid, which is Jesus Christ. Now if anyone builds on the foundation with gold, silver, precious stones, wood, hay, straw — each one's work will become manifest, for the Day will disclose it, because it will be revealed by fire, and the fire will test what sort of work each one has done. If the work that anyone has built on the foundation survives, he will receive a reward. If anyone's work is burned up, he will suffer loss, though he himself will be saved, but only as through fire" (I Corinthians 3:10-15).

The uncertainty of the time of Christ's Return together with the certainty of the fact of that event should drive mankind to prepare for it and the judgement invariably associated with it, and encourage Christians toward godliness and service

> *"Since everything will be destroyed in this way, what kind of people ought you to be? You ought to live holy and godly lives . . ."* (II Peter 3:11). (NIV)

> *"For we must all appear before the judgment seat of Christ, so that each one may receive what is due for what he has done in the body, whether good or evil"* (II Corinthians 5:10; II Thessalonians 1:5; Luke 21:27; Romans 8:23, Luke 19:13 and I Corinthians 3:10).

Presbyterians generally would be amillenial or postmillenial in their understanding of the millenium rather than premillenial. The first two views, amillenialism and postmillenialism, arise from a reformed and covenant view of Scripture as a whole. Premillenialism tends to have its roots in a dispensational perception of Scripture.

JUDGEMENT

DEATH AND BEYOND

The Bible is clear about mankind's fate after life. Mankind is a two-part being made up of body and soul or spirit. At death, the body returns to the earth, from which it originally came, and then decays

> *"By the sweat of your face you shall eat bread, till you return to the ground, for out of it you were taken; for you are dust, and to dust you shall return"* (Genesis 3:19).

> *"For David, after he had served the purpose of God in his own generation, fell asleep and was laid with his fathers and saw corruption"* (Acts 13:36).

At death the soul, being immortal, returns to God

> *". . . and the dust returns to the earth as it was, and the spirit returns to God who gave it"* (Ecclesiastes 12:7).

DEATH FOR THE BELIEVER

At death, the souls of believers, the righteous in Christ, are received immediately into heaven, enjoy fellowship with Christ and wait for the freeing of their bodies from corruption. Jesus promises the dying thief that he will be with Him that very day in heaven

> *"And he said to him, 'Truly, I say to you, today you will be with me in Paradise'"* (Luke 23:43).

Jesus speaks with warm comfort to His disciples about the prospect of heaven for themselves. Heaven is like a large home belonging to God the Father. There is ample space in it for all Jesus' followers: it has many rooms. Indeed, Jesus Himself is leaving them now, specifically to prepare a place for them and will personally return to bring them to heaven

> *"'Let not your hearts be troubled. Believe in God; believe also in me. In my Father's house are many rooms. If it were not so, would I have told you that I go to prepare a place for you? And if I go and prepare a place for you, I will come again and will take you to myself, that where I am you may be also . . .'"* (John 14:1-3).

Paul is sure that, when the tent of his body is dismantled, he has an eternal dwelling-place with God in heaven; so, for him, to be absent from the body is to be present with the Lord. Thus, Paul's most profound desire is to leave this life and to be with Christ, which is far better.

> *"For we know that if the tent that is our earthly home is destroyed, we have a building from God, a house not made with hands, eternal in the heavens"* (II Corinthians 5:1; II Corinthians 5:6, 7, 8; Philippians 1:23-25)

The writer to the Hebrews describes those who are in heaven as the *"spirits of righteous men made perfect"* (Hebrews 12:23) (NIV).

> "On the day of judgement the righteous, being gathered up to Christ in the clouds shall be placed

> on his right hand and there openly acknowledged and acquitted. They shall join with him in the judging of reprobate angels and men, and shall be received into heaven. There they shall be fully and for ever freed from all sin and misery, filled with inconceivable joys, made perfectly holy and happy both in body and in soul in the company of innumerable saints and holy angels, but especially in the immediate vision and enjoyment of God the Father, of our Lord Jesus Christ and of the Holy Spirit to all eternity. This is the perfect and full communion which the members of the invisible church shall enjoy with Christ in glory at the resurrection and day of judgement" (L.C. 90).

DEATH FOR THE UNBELIEVER

At death, the souls of unbelievers, the wicked outside Christ, face a very different prospect. They are sent to hell, remain in torment, reserved for judgement at the last day, when Christ returns. Jesus describes the rich man, after death, in hell and in torment

> *"In hell, where he was in torment, he looked up and saw Abraham far away, with Lazarus by his side. So he called to him, 'Father Abraham, have pity on me and send Lazarus to dip the tip of his finger in water and cool my tongue, because I am in agony in this fire'"* (Luke 16:23-24). (NIV)

Judas goes *"to where he belongs"* (Acts 1:25). Jude portrays fallen angels as kept in darkness, bound with everlasting chains for judgement on the great Day

> *"And the angels who did not stay within their own position of authority, but left their proper dwelling, he has kept in eternal chains under gloomy darkness until the judgment of the great day —"* (Jude 6).

Peter recalls their fate with fearful similarity, as sent to hell, put into gloomy dungeons to be held for judgement

> *"For if God did not spare angels when they sinned, but cast them into hell and committed them to chains*

> *of gloomy darkness to be kept until the judgment;"* (II Peter 2:4).

> "On the day of judgment the wicked shall be placed at Christ's left hand and, on clear evidence and full conviction of their own consciences, shall have the fearful, but just sentence of condemnation pronounced upon them. Following this they will be cast into hell away from the presence of God's favour and the glorious fellowship with Christ, his saints and all his holy angels. In hell, along with the devil and his angels, they will be punished for ever with unspeakable torments in both body and soul" (L.C. 89).

LIFE AFTER DEATH

The souls of both believer and unbeliever have conscious existence after death. They neither die nor sleep. The former are absorbed in the enjoyment of their Saviour; the latter are consumed with grief at the prospect of their coming Judge. Besides heaven and hell, Scripture describes no other ultimate destiny. There are no biblical grounds for purgatory, where souls are refined and purified for heaven, or for Limbus Patrum where Old Testament believers await Christ, or for Limbus Infantum where unbaptised children reside, or "soul-sleep" an unconscious end there after death. The Bible speaks only of heaven and hell.

SUMMARY

The Last Things

1. List some key words to describe important features of the second coming of Christ.

   _____

   _____

   _____

2. What are the main differences between the first and second coming of Christ?

   _____

   _____

   _____

3. List some of the events and trends in society that will occur before the return of Christ.

   _____

   _____

   _____

4. Describe briefly the main features of the three interpretations of the millennium.

   _____

   _____

   _____

5. What are the implications of Christ's return both for the believer and the non believer?

   _____

   _____

   _____

CHAPTER 10

COVENANT

Covenant in the Bible recalls God's plan of salvation. In Old Testament days a covenant was a solemn and binding agreement between two parties, where each made the other promises. Sometimes it was between two equals like Jonathan and David, sometimes between a superior and inferior like a king and a conquered people. Frequently it was ratified by a blood-oath with the death of an animal. God uses this latter kind of covenant between a superior and inferior, to disclose his plan of salvation in the Bible.

INTRODUCED

God **introduced** his covenant with Adam. God promises Adam continued well-being if he obeys God. Here, it was a covenant of works or, perhaps better, a covenant of life. But Adam broke the covenant because he sinned. Yet, even in judgment, God promised the birth of a child, who would destroy the devil who had caused Adam to sin

> *"The Lord God took the man and put him in the garden of Eden to work it and keep it. And the Lord God commanded the man, saying, "You may surely eat of every tree of the garden, but of the tree of the knowledge of good and evil you shall not eat, for in the day that you eat of it you shall surely die"* (Genesis 2:15-17).

> *"I will put enmity between you and the woman, and between your offspring and her offspring; he shall bruise your head, and you shall bruise his heel."* (Genesis 3:15).

INITIATED

God **initiated** his covenant with Abraham. Here, it is a covenant of grace, for Abraham is called to trust God completely and to go on a journey not knowing the destination. God promises to Abraham a family, a land as his inheritance but, above all, that he would be Abraham's God and the God of his descendants. Indeed, through Abraham all mankind will be blessed by God.

> *"Now the Lord said to Abram, "Go from your country and your kindred and your father's house to the land that I will show you. And I will make of you a great nation, and I will bless you and make your name great, so that you will be a blessing. I will bless those who bless you, and him who dishonours you I will curse, and in you all the families of the earth shall be blessed"* (Genesis 12:1-3).
>
> *"When Abram was ninety-nine years old the Lord appeared to Abram and said to him, 'I am God Almighty; walk before me, and be blameless, that I may make my covenant between me and you, and may multiply you greatly.'*
>
> *Then Abram fell on his face. And God said to him, 'Behold, my covenant is with you, and you shall be the father of a multitude of nations. No longer shall your name be called Abram, but your name shall be Abraham, for I have made you the father of a multitude of nations.*
>
> *I will make you exceedingly fruitful, and I will make you into nations, and kings shall come from you.*
>
> *And I will establish my covenant between me and you and your offspring after you throughout their generations for an everlasting covenant, to be God to you and to your offspring after you.*
>
> *And I will give to you and to your offspring after you the land of your sojournings, all the land of Canaan,*

Covenant

> *for an everlasting possession, and I will be their God'"* (Genesis 17:1-8).

CONFIRMED

God **confirmed** his covenant with Moses. God had redeemed Israel from slavery in Egypt by the blood of a slaughtered lamb. He had led them miraculously through the Red Sea, destroyed their enemies, given them his Law on Sinai and would lead them to the promised land. God had done all this for them because of the oath he had sworn to their forefathers

> *"It was not because you were more in number than any other people that the Lord set his love on you and chose you, for you were the fewest of all peoples, but it is because the Lord loves you and is keeping the oath that he swore to your fathers, that the Lord has brought you out with a mighty hand and redeemed you from the house of slavery, from the hand of Pharaoh king of Egypt. Know therefore that the Lord your God is God, the faithful God who keeps covenant and steadfast love with those who love him and keep his commandments, to a thousand generations . . ."* (Deuteronomy 7:7-9).

If Israel would keep God's covenant, they would be his treasured possession, his very own people

> *"Now therefore, if you will indeed obey my voice and keep my covenant, you shall be my treasured possession among all peoples, for all the earth is mine; and you shall be to me a kingdom of priests and a holy nation. These are the words that you shall speak to the people of Israel"* (Exodus 19:5, 6).

FORETOLD

God **foretold** his covenant through David. David would not build God's temple for he was a man of war. His son, rather, would do this. But God would never take away his steadfast covenant love from David or from his dynasty. There would always be a man to sit on the throne of Judah. God would establish the throne of his kingdom for ever. God would be his father, he would be God's son,

> "... from the time that I appointed judges over my people Israel. And I will give you rest from all your enemies. Moreover, the Lord declares to you that the Lord will make you a house. When your days are fulfilled and you lie down with your fathers, I will raise up your offspring after you, who shall come from your body, and I will establish his kingdom. He shall build a house for my name, and I will establish the throne of his kingdom forever. I will be to him a father, and he shall be to me a son. When he commits iniquity, I will discipline him with the rod of men, with the stripes of the sons of men, but my steadfast love will not depart from him, as I took it from Saul, whom I put away from before you. And your house and your kingdom shall be made sure forever before me. Your throne shall be established forever" (II Samuel 7:11-16).

Here, God forecasts the coming of the Messiah, the child to be born, the Mediator of the covenant, who would eventually be born of David's line.

EXPLAINED

God **explained** his covenant through the prophets.

Isaiah speaks of the *person* of the covenant. A child will be born who is human yet divine. He will be a king, who will rule on David's throne. His power of government will be increasing. His reign will never end. He will establish God's kingdom with justice and righteousness. God will bring this about

> "For to us a child is born, to us a son is given; and the government shall be upon his shoulder, and his name shall be called Wonderful Counsellor, Mighty God, Everlasting Father, Prince of Peace.

Covenant

> *Of the increase of his government and of peace there will be no end, on the throne of David and over his kingdom, to establish it and to uphold it with justice and with righteousness from this time forth and forevermore. The zeal of the Lord of hosts will do this"* (Isaiah 9:6, 7).

Jeremiah tells of the *work* of the covenant. God will make a new covenant with Israel and Judah, unlike the covenant they broke at Sinai. It will involve regeneration. God will put his law in their minds and write it on their hearts. It will mean revelation. They will all know God from the least of them to the greatest. It will bring remission of sins. God will forgive their wickedness and remember their sins no more. Truly, God will be their God and they will be his people

> *"'Behold, the days are coming, declares the Lord, when I will make a new covenant with the house of Israel and the house of Judah, not like the covenant that I made with their fathers on the day when I took them by the hand to bring them out of the land of Egypt, my covenant that they broke, though I was their husband, declares the Lord. But this is the covenant that I will make with the house of Israel after those days, declares the Lord: I will put my law within them, and I will write it on their hearts. And I will be their God, and they shall be my people. And no longer shall each one teach his neighbor and each his brother, saying, 'Know the Lord,' for they shall all know me, from the least of them to the greatest, declares the Lord. For I will forgive their iniquity, and I will remember their sin no more'"* (Jeremiah 31:31-34).

FULFILLED

God **fulfilled** his covenant in Christ.

The ***birth*** of Christ was in accordance with God's covenant. Mary thanks God that he has helped his servant Israel, remembering to be merciful to Abraham and his descendants for ever as he said to the fathers

> *"He has helped his servant Israel, in remembrance of his mercy, as he spoke to our fathers, to Abraham and to his offspring forever"* (Luke 1:54, 55).

The **death** of Christ was related to the covenant. Jesus describes his blood as that of the new covenant poured out for many for the forgiveness of sins

> *"for this is my blood of the covenant, which is poured out for many for the forgiveness of sins"* (Matthew 26:28).

> *"And likewise the cup after they had eaten, saying, 'This cup that is poured out for you is the new covenant in my blood'"* (Luke 22:20).

The **resurrection** of Christ came about as a result of the covenant. The writer of the Hebrews recalls the God of peace, who brought back from the dead our Lord Jesus through the blood of the eternal covenant

> *"Now may the God of peace who brought again from the dead our Lord Jesus, the great shepherd of the sheep, by the blood of the eternal covenant . . ."* (Hebrews 13:20).

The whole spectrum of Christ's earthly existence, birth, death and resurrection was bound up with God's covenant of grace.

APPLIED

God **applied** the truth of his covenant through the teaching of the apostles.

The writer to the Hebrews honours the *person* of the covenant. Jesus has become the guarantee of a better covenant. He is the mediator of a new covenant that those who are called may receive the promised eternal inheritance - now that he has died to set them free from the sins committed under the first

Covenant

covenant.

> *"Because of this oath, Jesus has become the guarantee of a better covenant"* (Hebrews 7:22) (NIV).

> *"Therefore he is the mediator of a new covenant, so that those who are called may receive the promised eternal inheritance, since a death has occurred that redeems them from the transgressions committed under the first covenant"* (Hebrews 9:15).

Paul explains the *work* of the covenant. Christ has redeemed us from the curse of the law by becoming a curse for us. He redeemed us in order that the blessing given to Abraham might come to the Gentiles through Christ Jesus, so that by faith we might receive the promise of the Spirit.

> *"Christ redeemed us from the curse of the law by becoming a curse for us — for it is written, "Cursed is everyone who is hanged on a tree" — so that in Christ Jesus the blessing of Abraham might come to the Gentiles, so that we might receive the promised Spirit through faith"* (Galatians 3:13, 14).

John records the *climax* of the covenant. He hears a voice from heaven saying,

> *"Behold, the dwelling place of God is with man. He will dwell with them, and they will be his people, and God himself will be with them as their God.*

> *The one who conquers will have this heritage, and I will be his God and he will be my son"*
> (Revelation 21:3, 7).

Throughout the Bible, from Genesis to Revelation God reveals his plan to save man through a covenant of grace. God approaches sinful man to draw him to faith in his Son, the Lord Jesus Christ, the covenant Head and Mediator. Sinful man receives Christ by faith as Saviour and so is saved from sin, becomes a child of God, inherits salvation and is brought within this personal possessive relationship with God: God is his Father, he is God's son. The plan of God is realized in his life.

"Father of peace, and God of love!
We own Thy power to save,
That power by which our Shepherd rose
Victorious o'er the grave.
Him from the dead Thou brought'st again,
When, by his sacred blood,
Confirmed and sealed for evermore,
The eternal covenant stood.
O may Thy Spirit seal our souls,
And mould them to Thy will,
That our weak hearts no more may stray
But keep Thy precepts still;
That to perfection's sacred height
We nearer still may rise,
And all we think, and all we do,
Be pleasing in Thine eyes"
(Paraphrase 60).

"By the fall the human race made itself incapable of life by that covenant, and so the Lord was pleased to make a second, commonly called the covenant of grace. In this covenant he freely offers to sinners life and salvation by Jesus Christ, requiring of them faith in Jesus Christ that they may be saved, and he promises to give his Holy Spirit to all those who are ordained to life to make them willing and able to believe" (W.C. 7:3).

SUMMARY

Covenant

1. What is a covenant?

2. What are the main features of God's covenant with Abraham, Moses, David and the Prophets? Think of your answer in terms of divine promise and our response.

3. Describe how God fulfils His covenant in Christ.

4. List some of the benefits of the better covenant in Christ.

CHAPTER 11

THE BIBLE

The Bible is the foundation of all we know about God. For that reason, it is a very special book. It is God's book. It is true that we can know a certain amount about God from nature

> *"The heavens declare the glory of God, and the sky above proclaims his handiwork. Day to day pours out speech, and night to night reveals knowledge. There is no speech, nor are there words, whose voice is not heard. Their voice goes out through all the earth, and their words to the end of the world. In them he has set a tent for the sun, which comes out like a bridegroom leaving his chamber, and, like a strong man, runs its course with joy. Its rising is from the end of the heavens, and its circuit to the end of them, and there is nothing hidden from its heat"* (Psalm 19:1-6 cf Psalm 19:7-11).

> *"For his invisible attributes, namely, his eternal power and divine nature, have been clearly perceived, ever since the creation of the world, in the things that have been made. So they are without excuse"* (Romans 1:20).

However, the view of God through the Bible is much better. Calvin said that reading the Bible is like spectacles to the elderly. It gives a much clearer picture of God than the hazy view through creation. The Bible is described as 'scripture'. Scripture means something 'written down'. The Bible gives a precise and permanent revelation of God. Three features of the Bible, above all, make this clear.

INSPIRED

The Bible is inspired. Paul wrote, *"All Scripture is breathed out by God"* (II Timothy 3:16). When we describe a painting or a poem as inspired, we mean it shows the artist's or the author's genius. But the inspiration of the Bible is even greater. Here, 'expired' would be better than 'inspired', for that is what Paul's term means. The Greek term *theopheustos,* literally God breathed, is used. Scripture is the words coming out of God's mouth, just as the little balloons in the children's comics contain the words of the speaker. Scripture is God speaking, breathing out words for our instruction.

Peter says the same thing, when he describes prophecy as men speaking from God, blown along by the Holy Spirit, just as a sailing ship is directed by the wind

> *"Above all, you must understand that no prophecy of Scripture came about by the prophet's own interpretation. For prophecy never had its origin in the will of man, but men spoke from God as they were carried along by the Holy Spirit"* (II Peter 1:20, 21). (NIV)

Jesus clearly identifies Scripture with God's words, for what scripture says, God says

> *"But he answered, "It is written,*
> *"'Man shall not live by bread alone, but by every word that comes from the mouth of God.'"*
>
> *Jesus said to him, "Again it is written, 'You shall not put the Lord your God to the test.'"*
>
> *Then Jesus said to him, "Be gone, Satan! For it is written,*
> *'You shall worship the Lord your God and him only shall you serve.'"* (Matthew 4:4, 7, 10).
>
> *"And he came to Nazareth, where he had been brought up. And as was his custom, he went to the synagogue on the Sabbath day, and he stood up to read. And the scroll of the prophet Isaiah was given to him. He unrolled the scroll and found the place where it was written,*
>
> *'The Spirit of the Lord is upon me, because he has anointed me to proclaim good news to the poor. He has sent me to proclaim liberty to the captives and*

The Bible

> *recovering of sight to the blind, to set at liberty those who are oppressed, to proclaim the year of the Lord's favor.'*
>
> *And he rolled up the scroll and gave it back to the attendant and sat down. And the eyes of all in the synagogue were fixed on him. And he began to say to them, 'Today this Scripture has been fulfilled in your hearing'"* (Luke 4:16-21).
>
> *"If he called them gods to whom the word of God came — and Scripture cannot be broken . . ."*
> (John 10:35).

All this, of course, refers specifically to the Old Testament, but New Testament is scripture too.

Peter calls Paul's letters scripture;

> *"And count the patience of our Lord as salvation, just as our beloved brother Paul also wrote to you according to the wisdom given him, as he does in all his letters when he speaks in them of these matters. There are some things in them that are hard to understand, which the ignorant and unstable twist to their own destruction, as they do the other Scriptures"* (II Peter 3:15-16).

Paul also quotes Luke 10: 7 as scripture

> *"For the Scripture says, 'You shall not muzzle an ox when it treads out the grain,' and, 'The laborer deserves his wages'"* (I Timothy 5:18; cf Deuteronomy 25:4 and Luke 10:7)

The process of inspiration continues from Old to New Testament.

This helps us not only to accept the Bible as God's word but also helps with the practical problem of what version or translation of the Bible to follow. We must assess the merits and demerits of each. Perhaps at the end of the day, we will study one or more versions to, gain the true meaning. But we must remember that no version is inspired. Scripture "as originally given" is inspired. Versions or translations are better or worse only as versions or translations of what originally is God-breathed. The Westminster Confession of Faith describes inspiration like this:

> "The Old Testament in Hebrew (which was the native language of the people of God of old), and the New Testament in Greek (which, at the time it was written, was the language most generally known among the nations), are immediately inspired by God. By his special care and providence, God has preserved them in purity ever since, so that they are authoritative . . ." (W.C. 1:8).

This section goes on to encourage translation into the ordinary language of the people, but it insists that the Bible is God's inspired word and, for that reason, authoritative.

ACCURATE

The Bible is accurate. Jesus said,

> "I tell you the truth, until heaven and earth disappear, not the smallest letter, not the least stroke of a pen, will by any means disappear from the Law until everything is accomplished"
> (Matthew 5:18). (NIV)

This is a remarkable statement. Can you spot the difference between the Hebrew spelling of Syria and Edom?

ארם = Syria   אדם = Edom –

there is only a tittle of a difference.

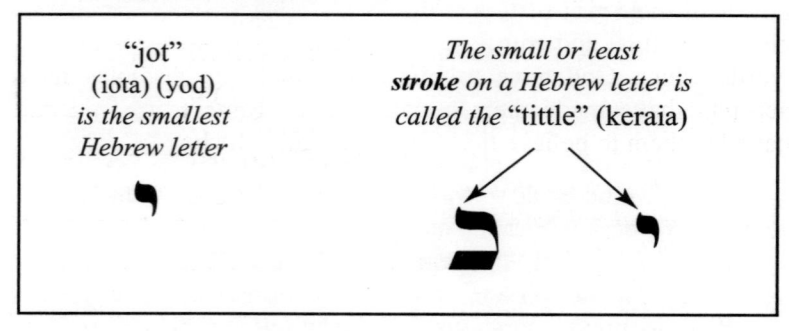

"jot"
(iota) (yod)
*is the smallest
Hebrew letter*

י

The small or least
stroke *on a Hebrew letter is
called the* "tittle" (keraia)

The Bible

The word "jot" (iota in the Greek New Testament) or ('yod') in Hebrew, is the smallest Hebrew letter.

The 'stroke of a pen' describes (keraia in Greek) the horn or the smallest/least stroke on some Hebrew letters. Jesus accepts the accuracy of scripture such that, to put it in our language, the dot on every letter 'i' and the stroke on every letter 't' will be fulfilled. This is why Jesus says quite categorically; *"and Scripture cannot be broken"* (John 10:35).

Today there is a view which accepts the Bible as accurate in matters of religion but not necessarily in other fields such as science, geography, history, biology or any other subject. But we must begin thinking from Jesus' estimate of scripture. Scripture is God's word. It is completely correct, absolutely accurate. Its authority is to be taken seriously for this reason: God is its author. Scripture is not only inspired but infallible and inerrant as well. Eventually written down by man, God originates its propositions and statements. God formulates what scripture says.

> *"The authority of the Holy Scripture does not depend on human testimony or a church's witness but entirely on God its author, who is truth itself. Therefore Holy Scripture is to be received, believed and obeyed because it is the word of God"* (W.C. 1:4).

SUFFICIENT

The Bible is sufficient. Scripture is sufficient under the power of the Spirit of God, its author, to bring us knowledge of God. It is final and complete in that sense. Jesus claims that the words which God gave to him and which his disciples have accepted have made them certain that he came from God and have led them to believe that God sent him,

> *"For I have given them the words that you gave me, and they have received them and have come to know in truth that I came from you; and they have believed that you sent me"* (John 17:8).

Paul assures Timothy that the scriptures, which he has

known from infancy, are able to make him wise about salvation through faith in Jesus Christ and that these same scriptures, being God-breathed, are useful for teaching, rebuking, correcting and training in righteousness so that the man of God may be thoroughly equipped for every good work

> *". . . and how from childhood you have been acquainted with the sacred writings, which are able to make you wise for salvation through faith in Christ Jesus. All Scripture is breathed out by God and profitable for teaching, for reproof, for correction, and for training in righteousness, that the man of God may be competent, equipped for every good work"* (II Timothy 3:15-17).

The scriptures lead to faith and produce growth in faith.

Peter describes the word preached in Asia Minor as a scriptural word, the living and enduring word of God, in fact, imperishable seed, through which his hearers have been born again

> *"since you have been born again, not of perishable seed but of imperishable, through the living and abiding word of God; for*
>
> > *'All flesh is like grass and all its glory like the flower of grass. The grass withers, and the flower falls, but the word of the Lord remains forever.'*
>
> *And this word is the good news that was preached to you"* (I Peter 1:23-25).

James asserts that God chooses to give birth through the word of truth so that Christians are a kind of first fruits or new species of all he created

> *"Of his own will he brought us forth by the word of truth, that we should be a kind of first fruits of his creatures"* (James 1:18).

So faith comes by hearing and hearing by the word of Christ

The Bible

> *"So faith comes from hearing, and hearing through the word of Christ"* (Romans 10:17).

Many problems arise today because the sufficiency of Scripture is not accepted. Some claim to have a message from God, that is, direct revelation. Certainly, we can be impressed by God's word to us at a particular juncture, but this must arise from the scriptural record already given, for example, from our daily Bible readings or the scriptures as expounded to us. But to seek fresh communication from God apart from scripture is a slight on the Spirit's work of revelation in scripture. Just as the living Word, Jesus Christ, is God's final message to us so also the written word, the Bible, is final confirmation of that message

> *"Long ago, at many times and in many ways, God spoke to our fathers by the prophets, but in these last days he has spoken to us by his Son, whom he appointed the heir of all things, through whom also he created the world"* (Hebrews 1:1, 2).
>
> *". . . and how from childhood you have been acquainted with the sacred writings, which are able to make you wise for salvation through faith in Christ Jesus. All Scripture is breathed out by God and profitable for teaching, for reproof, for correction, and for training in righteousness, that the man of God may be competent, equipped for every good work"* (II Timothy 3:15, 16, 17).

cf

> *"But even if we or an angel from heaven should preach to you a gospel contrary to the one we preached to you, let him be accursed. As we have said before, so now I say again: If anyone is preaching to you a gospel contrary to the one you received, let him be accursed"* (Galatians 1:8, 9; II Thessalonians 2:2).

Scripture is sufficient to bring to faith and to teach the believers within his faith.

> *"The whole will of God concerning all things*

necessary for his own glory, and for our salvation, faith and life, is either expressly stated in Scripture, or by good and necessary reasoning may be deduced from Scripture. Nothing, whether new revelations of the Spirit or human traditions, is ever to be added to Scripture . . ." (W.C. 1:6).

How we should love, treasure and obey the Bible, for the Bible is God's inspired, accurate and sufficient word. It alone brings us full knowledge of God and of his salvation.

SUMMARY

The Bible

1. Scripture, as originally given, is inspired. What does that mean?

2. The inspiration and divine authority of scripture was endorsed by Jesus and the Apostles. What, then, should be our attitude when we read the Bible?

3. List the main benefits of scripture for each humble recipient of its message.

CHAPTER 12

WORSHIP

MEANING OF WORSHIP

Collins Dictionary and Thesaurus defines "Worship" the noun as: adoration, homage, honour, regard, respect, reverence and the verb as: adore, edify, honour, idolize, love, respect, revere, reverence, venerate. There is plainly the sense in religion of giving God his worth in all this – his "worth-ship" or "worship". The Bible words for "worship" reflect the same meaning. There are two main categories here: The Old Testament Hebrew ABODAH and the New Testament Greek LATREIA mean "labour", "service". The Old Testament Hebrew SHACHAH and the New Testament Greek PROSKUNEO mean "bowing, bending the knee", "paying homage, honouring the worth of someone". There is both adoration and activity in Biblical worship. Indeed, from these words and their use in the Bible, there is the general sense in which worship includes the whole of the believer's life as adoring service of God and the specific sense in which believers gather together to honour God and give him his worth at particular times.

MODES OF WORSHIP

OLD TESTAMENT

Individual Worship

As God revealed himself in Old Testament times, individuals responded not only in general terms by serving God in daily life but in specific terms by meeting with him as a result of his self-revelation to them. We find this in the experience of Adam and Eve, Noah, Abraham, Jacob, Moses and Isaiah to name but a few. This activity is described at the outset of the

Bible in these terms:

> *"At that time people began to call upon the name of the Lord"* (Genesis 4:26).

This indicates man's recognition of God as God, his expressed need of God and his obedience to God. It is an adoration and an activity, which we might call individual worship. This stresses the believer's personal relationship with God as of fundamental and continuing importance.

Covenant Worship

As God develops his covenant relationship with Abraham and his children, worship takes on a covenantal aspect. By the time of Moses, the Ten Commandments require man's obedience to God's revealed Law. This Law is to be assiduously taught to successive generations of children within the covenant community. Israel is required to appear three times annually before the Lord as a QAHAL or "congregation" of Jehovah. The reading and teaching of the written Law of God is an important element in Israel's on-going instruction. Priests and scribes are committed to this task. Education in the Law or Word of God is a constituent part of God's covenant relationship with his people. Covenantal worship anticipates the corporate relationship of God with his people in New Testament times and today. The QAHAL, "congregation" or "called together ones" of the Old Testament becomes the EKKLESIA, "church" or "called out ones" of the New Testament. The teaching and subsequent understanding of the Law or Word of God is fundamental to worship in both Testaments.

Sacrificial Worship

Sacrificial worship is pointedly evident in the Old Testament. The time, place and actions of sacrifice are stressed. Sacrifice daily, morning and evening, weekly on the Sabbath, monthly at the New Moon Feasts and annually at the yearly festivals marks the continuum of this form of worship. The place was originally the Tabernacle and eventually the Temple. Sacrifice offered elsewhere was contrary to God's Law. The modes of sacrifice included burnt and whole burnt offering, meal offering, peace offering, sin and guilt offering. These actions, in all, required the necessary death of the sin-bearing victim, if sin was to be properly dealt with and a covenant relationship with God effectively maintained:

> *"Without the shedding of blood there is no forgiveness"* (Hebrews 9:22).

This principle becomes clear in statements regarding the observance of sacrifice in Leviticus:

> *"Moses took the blood, and with his finger put it on the horns of the altar around it and purified the altar and poured out the blood at the base of the altar and consecrated it to make atonement for it"* (Leviticus 8:15).
>
> *"For the life of the flesh is in the blood, and I have given it for you on the altar to make atonement for your souls, for it is the blood that makes atonement by the life"* (Leviticus 17:11).

Priests and Levites were to carry out these duties in accordance with the prescribed rules of God's Law. While mere ceremonialism or formalism were stringently rejected,[7] and, the main point of the whole sacrificial worship in the Old Testament was to anticipate the finality of Christ's own

---

[7] *"In sacrifice and offering you have not delighted, but you have given me an open ear. Burnt offering and sin offering you have not required"* (Psalms 40:6 cf Psalms 50:7-15).

"'With what shall I come before the Lord, and bow myself before God on high? Shall I come before him with burnt offerings, with calves a year old? Will the Lord be pleased with thousands of rams, with ten thousands of rivers of oil? Shall I give my firstborn for my transgression, the fruit of my body for the sin of my soul?' He has told you, O man, what is good; and what does the Lord require of you but to do justice, and to love kindness, and to walk humbly with your God?" (Micah 6:6-8).

sacrifice as an end of animal sacrificial worship.[8]

NEW TESTAMENT

FULFILMENT

Jesus fulfils Old Testament worship whether viewed from the specific or general point of view. Jesus is the ultimate sacrifice to end all animal sacrifices (Hebrews 10:18). Such spiritual sacrifices acceptable to God through Jesus Christ, as the New Testament mentions, are clearly of a non-animal variety and include consecrated Christian living as evident in praise, good works and sharing with others

> *"you yourselves like living stones are being built up as a spiritual house, to be a holy priesthood, to offer spiritual sacrifices acceptable to God through Jesus Christ"* (I Peter 2:5).

> *"I appeal to you therefore, brothers, by the mercies of God, to present your bodies as a living sacrifice, holy and acceptable to God, which is your spiritual worship"* (Romans 12:1; Hebrews 13:15,16).

Jesus is the Great High Priest not of the order of Levi but of Melchisedek, a priest who acts

> *"not on the basis of a regulation as to his ancestry but on the basis of the power of an indestructible life" "... but because Jesus lives forever, he has a permanent priesthood"* (Hebrews 7:16, 24). (NIV)

He is the true Tabernacle and Temple

> *"Jesus answered them, "Destroy this temple, and in three days I will raise it up." The Jews then said, "It has taken forty-six years to build this temple, and*

---

[8] *"Where there is forgiveness of these, there is no longer any offering for sin"* (Hebrews 10:18).

Worship

> *will you raise it up in three days?" But he was speaking about the temple of his body. When therefore he was raised from the dead, his disciples remembered that he had said this, and they believed the Scripture and the word that Jesus had spoken"*
> (John 2:19-22; 1:14).

He is Lord of the Sabbath,

> *"And he said to them, 'Have you never read what David did, when he was in need and was hungry, he and those who were with him: how he entered the house of God, in the time of Abiathar the high priest, and ate the bread of the Presence, which it is not lawful for any but the priests to eat, and also gave it to those who were with him?' And he said to them, 'The Sabbath was made for man, not man for the Sabbath. So the Son of Man is lord even of the Sabbath'"* (Mark 2:25-28).

He is the focal part of the annual Jewish feasts:

the Passover Lamb,

> *"The next day he saw Jesus coming toward him, and said, 'Behold, the Lamb of God, who takes away the sin of the world!'"* (John 1:29).

> *"Cleanse out the old leaven that you may be a new lump, as you really are unleavened. For Christ, our Passover lamb, has been sacrificed"*
> (I Corinthians 5:7).

the Day of Atonement, (Hebrews 10:9-14)

the Feast of Tabernacles,

> *"And the Word became flesh and dwelt among us, and we have seen his glory, glory as of the only Son from the Father, full of grace and truth"* (John 1:14).

> *"On the last day of the feast, the great day, Jesus stood up and cried out, "If anyone thirsts, let him come to me and drink. Whoever believes in me, as*

> the Scripture has said, 'Out of his heart will flow rivers of living water'" (John 7:37, 38).

for **Jesus is the mediator of a new covenant,**

> "Therefore he is the mediator of a new covenant, so that those who are called may receive the promised eternal inheritance, since a death has occurred that redeems them from the transgressions committed under the first covenant" (Hebrews 9:15; Hebrews 12:22-29).

In this sense, Jesus both fulfils and abolishes these aspects of Old Testament worship.

CONTINUITY

There is however, continuity between Old Testament and New Testament worship both specifically and generally.

Jesus promises to be with the two or three who come together in his name and, indeed, to answer prayer in such a context

> "Again I say to you, if two of you agree on earth about anything they ask, it will be done for them by my Father in heaven. For where two or three are gathered in my name, there am I among them" (Matthew 18:19, 20).

Jesus chooses the twelve to be with him, who later are given leadership within the Church

> "And he appointed twelve (whom he also named apostles) so that they might be with him and he might send them out to preach" (Mark 3:14).

This leadership includes a function of acting as judges and

Worship

rulers of God's people,[9] with power to bind and loose,[10] to remit and to retain sins.[11] This is described as the "keys of the kingdom". The keys are both of doctrine in teaching what conduct is permitted and what is forbidden and of discipline in removing those unworthy and restoring the contrite. The leadership is seen within a corporate context in matters of dispute (Matthew 18:18).

Jesus establishes the church on the foundation of Peter's confession of him as Christ, the Son of the living God[12] and commissions the apostles to disciple all nations in precise terms of baptising and teaching.

> *"Go therefore and make disciples of all nations, baptizing them in the name of the Father and of the Son and of the Holy Spirit, teaching them . . ."*
> (Matthew 28:19, 20).

Though the worship of the Jews was correct in its understanding as over against that of the Samaritans, Jesus further makes it plain that worship is no longer specifically local or purely formal but now, since he has come, "in spirit and in truth" (John 4:21-24).

Luke records how those baptized on the Day of Pentecost were added to the number of the church and how, from the outset, believers devoted themselves to the apostles' teaching, to the

---

[9] *"Jesus said to them, 'Truly, I say to you, in the new world, when the Son of Man will sit on his glorious throne, you who have followed me will also sit on twelve thrones, judging the twelve tribes of Israel . . .'"* (Mathew 19:28).

[10] *"Truly, I say to you, whatever you bind on earth shall be bound in heaven, and whatever you loose on earth shall be loosed in heaven"* (Matthew 18:18).

[11] *"If you forgive the sins of any, they are forgiven them; if you withhold forgiveness from any, it is withheld"* (John 20:23).

[12] *"Simon Peter replied, 'You are the Christ, the Son of the living God'"* (Mathew 16:16).

fellowship, to the breaking of bread (probably referring to the sacraments of the Lord's Supper or Communion) and to prayer in a continuing setting of praise and mutual sharing.

> *"So those who received his word were baptized, and there were added that day about three thousand souls.*
>
> *And they devoted themselves to the apostles' teaching and the fellowship, to the breaking of bread and the prayers. And awe came upon every soul, and many wonders and signs were being done through the apostles. And all who believed were together and had all things in common. And they were selling their possessions and belongings and distributing the proceeds to all, as any had need. And day by day, attending the temple together and breaking bread in their homes, they received their food with glad and generous hearts, praising God and having favor with all the people. And the Lord added to their number day by day those who were being saved"*
> (Acts 2:41-47).

He recalls, too, how at Troas on the first day of the week believers came together to "break bread" and listened to Paul address them

> *"On the first day of the week, when we were gathered together to break bread, Paul talked with them, intending to depart on the next day, and he prolonged his speech until midnight"* (Acts 20:7).

Paul writes to the Corinthian church about meetings in which the church comes together to eat the Lord's Supper and to hear a hymn, word of instruction, revelation or prophecy in familiar languages as well as in God-given interpretation of utterances in unfamiliar languages. Here Paul insists that the guiding principle should be decency, order and intelligibility both on the part of speakers and hearers, including visiting unbelievers (I Corinthians 11:17-34; 14:1-39). Many in the reformed tradition, including the present writer, believe that such supernatural gifts as Paul

Worship

mentions here were given to the Church at its founding to attest the witness of the apostles and, with the completion of Scripture, are not to be expected today.

> *"Therefore we must pay much closer attention to what we have heard, lest we drift away from it. For since the message declared by angels proved to be reliable, and every transgression or disobedience received a just retribution, how shall we escape if we neglect such a great salvation? It was declared at first by the Lord, and it was attested to us by those who heard, while God also bore witness by signs and wonders and various miracles and by gifts of the Holy Spirit distributed according to his will"* (Hebrews 2:1-4).

> *"The signs of a true apostle were performed among you with utmost patience, with signs and wonders and mighty works"* (II Corinthians 12:12).

> *"built on the foundation of the apostles and prophets, Christ Jesus himself being the cornerstone"* (Ephesians 2:20).

The inference of church meetings for worship in which instruction and encouragement in the Word are to the fore is plausibly plain. Paul writes in his Pastoral letters to Timothy and Titus of the duties of church leaders regarding public prayer and the public reading, preaching and teaching of Scripture in such a way as to suggest meetings, where these activities were the norm.

> *"Command and teach these things. Let no one despise you for your youth, but set the believers an example in speech, in conduct, in love, in faith, in purity. Until I come, devote yourself to the public reading of Scripture, to exhortation, to teaching. Do not neglect the gift you have, which was given you by prophecy when the council of elders laid their hands on you. Practice these things, immerse yourself in them, so that all may see your progress. Keep a close watch on yourself and on the teaching. Persist in this, for by so doing you will save both yourself*

> *and your hearer"* (I Timothy 4:11-16; I Timothy 2:1-15 and II Timothy 1:13,14).

> *"You then, my child, be strengthened by the grace that is in Christ Jesus, and what you have heard from me in the presence of many witnesses entrust to faithful men who will be able to teach others also"* (II Timothy 2:1,2; II Timothy 3:10-4:5 and Titus 2:1-15).

Clearly, Old Testament priest appears to be replaced by New Testament presbyter in the office of church leadership

Paul also urges believers to let the word of Christ dwell richly in them as they teach and advise one another and as they sing psalms, hymns and spiritual songs in their hearts to God

> *"Let the word of Christ dwell in you richly, teaching and admonishing one another in all wisdom, singing psalms and hymns and spiritual songs, with thankfulness in your hearts to God"* (Colossians 3:16),

> *". . . addressing one another in psalms and hymns and spiritual songs, singing and making melody to the Lord with your heart"* (Ephesians 5:19).

Here praise would seem to be a part of these worship meetings. Some Presbyterians in the reformed tradition regard "psalms, hymns and spiritual songs" as three categories of the canonical psalms which alone should be used in worship: practice known as 'exclusive psalmody'. Others regard "hymns and spiritual songs" as human compositions outside the canonical Psalms which, in their opinion, may be used in worship.

The writer to the Hebrews urges his readers to spur one another on to love and good works, not to give up meeting together, as some are in the habit of doing but rather to encourage one another, all the more as they see the Day approaching (Hebrews 10:24, 25).

James warns of the danger of showing favouritism and paying special attention to the rich folk who come to their meetings,

Worship

> "Suppose a man comes into your meeting wearing a gold ring and fine clothes, and a poor man in shabby clothes also comes in. If you show special attention to the man wearing fine clothes and say, 'Here's a good seat for you,' but say to the poor man, 'You stand there,' or, 'Sit on the floor by my feet,' have you not discriminated among yourselves and become judges with evil thoughts?" (James 2: 2-4).

John records visions of worship in heaven, where the Glory of Jesus' as Lamb, King and Word is celebrated amid praises of elders, who appear to represent Old Testament tribes and New Testament apostles (Revelations 4:1- ; 5:14; 19:1-21).

The overall picture is that worship in the New Testament not only marked the entire fabric of Christian living in general but was evident in Christian meetings in particular. In these meetings the Word of God was paramount. The move from Old Testament to New Testament worship in the specific sense is a move from the elaborate ritual associated with the sacrificial system to relative simplicity. There is a kind of "ritual" in the New Testament, for example, in baptism and the Lord's Supper, but this in itself points up the contrast. New Testament worship is Christ-centred and Word-orientated. Instruction and encouragement in Scripture are its leading characteristics. It is Bible-based. Its meetings are marked by prayer, the reading and preaching of the Word, singing God's praise and possibly the observance of the Lord's Supper and perhaps baptism. This is plainly evident from the foregoing analysis and is well expressed in the words of the Westminster Confession:

> "The reading of the Scriptures with godly fear, the sound preaching and conscientious and obedient hearing of the word of God with understanding, faith, and reverence, the singing of psalms with grace in the heart, the due administration and worthy receiving of the sacraments instituted by Christ - these are all parts of the ordinary religious worship of God. In addition, religious oaths, vows, solemn fasting, and thanksgiving on special occasions, are to be used in a holy and reverent

manner at appropriate times" (WC 21:5).

MANDATE FOR WORSHIP

The mandate for worship is a vital issue. Is worship a matter of human concoction or divine prescription? The Presbyterian and reformed tradition have affirmed the latter, a feature known as the "regulative principle", that is, that the worship of God is dictated by what God prescribes in Scripture not what man thinks is suitable.

A quick glance at Scripture itself makes this position clear, whether worship is viewed from the broad perspective of life in general or from the narrow aspect of meeting with God in particular.

The Old Testament reflects this situation: Adam and Eve were free to eat the fruit of any tree in the garden of Eden but not of the tree of the knowledge of good and evil.

> *"And the Lord God commanded the man, saying, 'You may surely eat of every tree of the garden, but of the tree of the knowledge of good and evil you shall not eat, for in the day that you eat of it you shall surely die'"* (Genesis 2:16, 17).

Cain's offering, as over against that of Abel, was unacceptable to God.

> *"In the course of time Cain brought to the Lord an offering of the fruit of the ground, and Abel also brought of the firstborn of his flock and of their fat portions. And the Lord had regard for Abel and his offering, but for Cain and his offering he had no regard. So Cain was very angry, and his face fell"* (Genesis 4:3-5).

Aaron's sons Nadab and Abihu offered "unauthorised fire" before the Lord, contrary to his command. So fire from the Lord came and destroyed them.

Worship

> "Now Nadab and Abihu, the sons of Aaron, each took his censer and put fire in it and laid incense on it and offered unauthorized fire before the Lord, which he had not commanded them. And fire came out from before the Lord and consumed them, and they died before the Lord. Then Moses said to Aaron, "This is what the Lord has said, 'Among those who are near me I will be sanctified, and before all the people I will be glorified.'" And Aaron held his peace" (Leviticus 10:1-3).

Saul the king, impatient because Samuel the priest had not arrived, offered burnt and fellowship offerings against God's command and as a result, was deposed from office (II Samuel 13: 7-14).

Uzzah irreverently put his hand on the ark of God to steady it and was struck down in death.

> "And when they came to the threshing floor of Nacon, Uzzah put out his hand to the ark of God and took hold of it, for the oxen stumbled. And the anger of the Lord was kindled against Uzzah, and God struck him down there because of his error, and he died there beside the ark of God" (II Samuel 6: 6,7).

Jeroboam indulged in idolatry, built shrines at high places, appointed priests regularly and initiated a festival at Bethel. Consequently, he was condemned by a man of God, presumably a prophet, for his actions (I Kings 12:25–13:34). The first four of the Ten Commandments deal with worship in a number of ways: the first forbids the worship of false gods, the second forbids worship through idols, the third forbids the wrong use of God's holy name, the fourth requires remembrance of the Sabbath.

Condemnation of idolatry is repeated throughout the Bible. In the Old Testament to ignore God's specific commands brought the dire consequences of divine judgement.

The New Testament echoes the same note regarding worship

whether broadly or narrowly conceived. Negatively, Jesus condemns as false worship superficiality and hypocrisy which arise from human tradition[13] rather than from God's Word, quoting Isaiah the prophet as authority

> *"And the Lord said: 'Because this people draw near with their mouth and honour me with their lips, while their hearts are far from me, and their fear of me is a commandment taught by men . . .'"* (Isaiah 29:13).

Positively, Jesus commends Jewish over against Samaritan worship, but initiates a new regime of worshipping God altogether, God the Father in spirit and in truth (John 4:19-26). Paul reminds the church at Corinth that abuse of the Lord's Supper has serious consequences and warns Colossian believers against "self-imposed" or "will" worship based on human commands and teachings rather than God's word.

> *"If with Christ you died to the elemental spirits of the world, why, as if you were still alive in the world, do you submit to regulations — "Do not handle, Do not taste, Do not touch" (referring to things that all perish as they are used) — according to human precepts and teachings? These have indeed an appearance of wisdom in promoting self-made religion and asceticism and severity to the body, but they are of no value in stopping the indulgence of the flesh"* (Colossians 2:20-23; cf. I Corinthians 11:29-32).

---

[13] (Matthew 15: 1-9) *Then Pharisees and scribes came to Jesus from Jerusalem and said, "Why do your disciples break the tradition of the elders? For they do not wash their hands when they eat." He answered them, "And why do you break the commandment of God for the sake of your tradition? For God commanded, 'Honour your father and your mother,' and, 'Whoever reviles father or mother must surely die.' But you say, 'If anyone tells his father or his mother, "What you would have gained from me is given to God," he need not honour his father.' So for the sake of your tradition you have made void the word of God. You hypocrites! Well did Isaiah prophesy of you, when he said:*

> *"'This people honours me with their lips, but their heart is far from me; in vain do they worship me, teaching as doctrines the commandments of men.'"*

Worship

The writer to the Hebrews requires his readers to worship God acceptably with reverence and awe, for God is a consuming fire

> *"Therefore let us be grateful for receiving a kingdom that cannot be shaken, and thus let us offer to God acceptable worship, with reverence and awe, for our God is a consuming fire"* (Hebrews 12:28, 29),

cf

> *"For the Lord your God is a consuming fire, a jealous God"* (Deuteronomy 4:24).

The rule for worship and in both testaments is clearly mandated by God's prescription not by human opinion. The Bible dictates how God is to be worshipped. To ignore this is to call down divine judgement.

This "regulative principle", as it is known, is put positively by the Presbyterian and Reformed tradition: *'we may only do in worship what Scripture prescribes – whatever Scripture does not command is forbidden'.* Roman Catholics, Episcopalians and Lutherans express the principal negatively: *'we may do anything in worship except what Scripture forbids'.*

The Westminster Confession of Faith puts it this way:

> *"God's revelation in his works shows the existence of a God who has dominion and sovereignty over all, who is good and does good to all, and who is therefore to be feared, loved, praised, called on, trusted and served with all one's heart, with all one's soul and with all one's might. But the only acceptable way of worshipping the true God is appointed by himself in accordance with what he has revealed in his word. Therefore he is not to be worshipped according to human ideas or inventions, nor according to the suggestions of Satan, nor by means of visible representations, nor in any other way not prescribed in the Holy Scripture"* (WC 21:1).

The Westminster Confession, however, does recognise that there are certain aspects of the worship of God and the government of the church not particularly prescribed in Scripture.

Hence, the Confession allows for a somewhat different approach to such matters. It acknowledges that:

> "... there are some circumstances concerning the worship of God, and government of the Church, common to human actions and societies, which are to be ordered by the light of nature and Christian prudence, according to the general rules of the word, which are always to be observed" (WC 1:6).
> © "Confession of Faith and Subordinate Standards" The Free Church of Scotland

Within the reformed tradition there have been those who make a distinction between what has been described as the **elements of worship**, that is: prayer, thanksgiving, reading the Word, preaching, singing God's praises and administering the sacraments and the ***circumstances of worship** (and government of the church)*; such as: the time and place of meeting, the precise language to be used in prayer. Such a distinction can be seen as reasonable not only for worship in the specific but also in the general sense of the word as relating to the whole of the Christian life. There is no necessary discrepancy between these two sections in the Confession, and the rule of Scripture.

MATTERS OF WORSHIP
ATTITUDE

The primacy of Scripture and the regulative principle means that worship meetings ought to be Bible-oriented. Such worship meetings are prescribed by God through his Word not ordered by man through his opinions. However, this has largely been ignored in evangelism today. On the back of consumerist philosophy, large mega churches promote seeker friendly services whose purpose is to win the unconverted to Christ and whose primary motivation in the elements in worship is evangelism not the regulative principle. Those in the reformed tradition however believe that if Scripture is the means not only of converting sinners but also of sanctifying believers, then worship services ordered according to the Word will be far more effective in evangelism and, more importantly, in glorifying God. The primary object of worship is God not man. The Reformers

Worship

rightly regard religious feelings, or what the Puritans called "the religious affections" as being subject to the mind informed by Scripture. Paul is adamant that if unbelievers and those who do not understand, come into a Christian meeting and find worship services unintelligible, they will conclude that believers are out of their minds. On the other hand, if matters in the meeting are intelligible, they will fall down and worship God, exclaiming *"God is really among you!"* (I Corinthians 14: 22-25).[14]

Meetings in which the Bible is central – praying the Bible, singing the Bible, preaching the Bible, administering the Bible in sacramental signs and seals will, above all, promote this. The regulative principle works because Scripture is primary.

ACTIVITIES

Some activities in the modern worship scene present difficulties. Within Pentecostal Churches which dates from the beginning of the twentieth century and within charismaticism affecting mainline denominations and dating from the mid-twentieth century phenomena such as tongues or *glossalia*, in terms of no known semantic origin, prophecy representing direct revelation and miraculous healing have become widespread. If it happened in Bible churches, it should happen today, the argument runs. Reformed tradition, as already noted, have regarded such phenomena as confirmatory of the apostolic witness and ceasing with the completion of Scripture and therefore not to be expected in the Church today.

Also, under the influence of charismatism: drama, dance,

---

[14] *"Thus tongues are a sign not for believers but for unbelievers, while prophecy is a sign not for unbelievers but for believers. If, therefore, the whole church comes together and all speak in tongues, and outsiders or unbelievers enter, will they not say that you are out of your minds? But if all prophesy, and an unbeliever or outsider enters, he is convicted by all, he is called to account by all, the secrets of his heart are disclosed, and so, falling on his face, he will worship God and declare that God is really among you"*
(I Corinthians 14:22-25).

raising of hands and other activities such as spontaneous verbal responses of affirmation, clapping and manifestations of body language have been encouraged. While dramatic and hence 'mime' aspects are found in Scripture itself, in prophetic symbolism and within Jesus' teaching, the regulative principle would certainly suggest that all these aspects having been completed within Scripture means that the primary mode of communication must be verbal, namely preaching and teaching, which is aimed at informing and challenging the mind. Dance is mentioned in Scripture, but even there its association tends largely to be within paganism, and both then and today, even allowing for an emphasis on 'folk' rather than 'sexual orientation', the dominant note of criticism makes dance an inappropriate medium for worship. 'Lifting holy hands' as referred to in scripture has, we believe, more a metaphorical than physical meaning. It tends today to focus on emotional rather than mental activity, and is not entirely appropriate for worship in our view.

MUSIC

The other primary controversial aspect in today's worship scene is that of music particularly in its connection with the element of praise. It is often thought that the main feature of controversy here is the difference between 'traditional' and 'contemporary' praise, a difference which relates to the generation gap. While this is certainly one feature in the debate, it is not the only one and is sometimes a 'red herring' which distracts from a much more theological issue related to the regulative principal. In the event, while praise might be rightly regarded as an 'element' of worship, music is only a 'circumstance'.

For some sixteen centuries the main form of praise within Christianity was the canonical Psalms and, for quite a time within those centuries, this was unaccompanied. Presbyterians of the "Reformed" or "Covenanting" churches would maintain, in terms of the regulative principle, that praise ought to be exclusive unaccompanied psalmody; Psalms are the divinely inspired song book in the Bible, the "psalms, hymns and spiritual songs" mentioned in the New Testament representing three categories of canonical Psalms. With the fulfilment of Old Testament sacrificial worship in Christ, musical accompaniment should cease and unaccompanied Psalm singing, the purest form of praise, should be normative in the Christian Church, is the opinion of this particular branch of presbyterianism.

Other Protestant Churches, including some Presbyterian, would not go as far as exclusive unaccompanied psalmody. They include paraphrases or versified portions of Scripture other than the Psalms and hymns of human composition in worship and these being instrumentally accompanied. Their reasoning would be as follows: Scripture includes, apart from canonical Psalms, poetic and hymnic portions; solo, responsive and instrumental forms of praise.

The historic development of this is interesting. At various periods often associated with what would be called religious 'revival', diverse musical forms developed. At the Reformation, Calvinistic psalms, paraphrases of Scripture other than the Psalms and Lutheran hymns in the vernacular arose. Before and during the evangelical awakening of the eighteenth century, hymns by Isaac Watts, Charles Wesley and Augustine Toplady, were prevalent. The late nineteenth century witnessed an upsurge of evangelical music by such writers as Fanny Crosby, Ira Sankey, Frances Havergal and Philip Bliss. Following the second World War organisations seeking to influence youth, such as Youth for Christ added music associated with popular styles and since 1970, Scripture songs, choruses and some modern hymns have supplemented this development, a number of these associated with charismaticism.

Many Presbyterian and Christians of the older generation have resisted this development. It was criticized as lacking doctrinal substance, being too emotional, hyper-subjective and following secular musical idiom which produced a lack of reverence. Some of these criticisms are undoubtedly true. Justifiable criticism has also been levelled against extreme forms of instrumentation. Musical groups with guitars, drums or even more musically acceptable forms such as orchestral have tended to make music the main object of the worship. This has not only harmed the reverence and awe Scripture requires of worship but has displaced and sidelined the Word and its exposition which ought to be central and, indeed the motivation of all praise. To please and involve a 'younger generation' is no justification for this. In fact, it spoils and ruins within that younger generation a true appreciation of biblical worship. That generation needs education in true worship not encouragement in promoting false worship. Often the issue in praise within worship is not the so-called 'generation gap' at all but the far deeper problem of assessing the true purpose and nature of worship and the need to consider biblical principles and practice in determining the parameters of praise within worship.

Praise in the Bible seems to share two focal points: the glory of God and the encouragement of believers. For those who do not go as far as exclusive psalmody, these parameters must circumscribe hymn-writing. Biblically based, theologically rich, Christ-centred compositions are to be encouraged. Alongside the Scottish paraphrases of portions of Scripture, many modern Reformed hymn-writers such as Eric Alexander and James Montgomery Boice have done much to revive biblical praise in this field. Development in modern psalmody has also made excellent strides. A rediscovery of psalmody, an increase in composition of biblical paraphrases, a development of Reformed hymnody and a judicious use of praise from other sources seems to be the best way forward. Then we will be truly reformed and biblical church at worship.

Worship

SUMMARY

Worship

Worship in O.T. times, was led by Priests and Levites who were to carry out sacrificial duties in accordance with God's prescribed law.

1. What element was common to both the Old and New sacrifice? *(List your references)*.

   _____

   _____

2. When did this sacrificial system end?

   _____

   _____

3. Who was the last Priest?

   _____

   _____

4. How did this last Priest fulfil the Old Testament system? *(List your references)*.

   _____

   _____

5. How and when are we to worship today? cf. Acts 20:7 WC 21:1 *(List your references)*.

   _____

   _____

   _____

6. What are the main focal points which praise in the bible seem to share?

7. What does the Presbyterian Church teach regarding the "Regulative Principle"?

8. What does Paul say should be normal activities in a worship service?

Further Reading

For further reading:-

1. "A Journey in Grace" a theological novel, Richard P. Belcher, Evangelical Press, Faverdale North Industrial Estate, Darlington, Co. Durham, DL3 0PH, England, ISBN 0 85234 309 4

2. "The Momentous Event", A discussion of scripture teaching on the second advent, W.J.Grier, The Banner of Truth Trust, 3, Murrayfield Road, Edinburgh, EH12 6EL, P.O. Box 621, Carlisle, Pennsylvania, 17013, USA, ISBN 0 85151 020 5

3. "Whatever Happened to the Gospel of Grace? recovering the doctrines that shook the world", James Montgomery Boice, Crossway Books, 1300 Crescent Street, Wheaton, Illinois 60187, ISBN 1-58134-237-3

4. "John Owen on the Christian Life", Sinclair B. Ferguson, The Banner of Truth Trust, 3, Murrayfield Road, Edinburgh, EH12 6EL, P.O. Box 621, Carlisle, Pennsylvania, 17013, USA, ISBN 0 85151 503 7

5. "The Mystery of Providence", John Flavel, The Banner of Truth Trust, 3, Murrayfield Road, Edinburgh, EH12 6EL, P.O. Box 621, Carlisle, Pennsylvania, 17013, USA, ISBN 0 85151 104 X

6. "This little church went to market", Gary Gilley, Evangelical Press, Faverdale North Industrial Estate, Darlington, Co. Durham, DL3 0PH, England, ISBN 0 85234 596 8

7. "This little church stayed at home", Gary Gilley, Evangelical Press, Faverdale North Industrial Estate, Darlington, Co. Durham, DL3 0PH, England, ISBN 0 85234 603 4

8. "The Last Things, Death, Judgement, Heaven and Hell", Paul Helm, The Banner of Truth Trust, 3, Murrayfield Road, Edinburgh, EH12 6EL, P.O. Box 621, Carlisle, Pennsylvania, 17013, USA, ISBN 0 85151 544 4

9. "Worship in the Melting Pot", Peter Masters 2002, The Wakeman Trust, 38, Walcot Square, London, SE11 4TZ, ISBN 1 870855 337

10. "Firm Foundations, A Faith for today's Church, A study manual on the Westminster Confession of Faith", William McKeown, Published by the Board of Evangelism and Christian Training, The Presbyterian Church in Ireland, Church House, Fisherwick Place, Belfast, BT1 6DW, Northern Ireland

11. "A Case for Amillennialism Understanding the End Times", Kim Riddlebarger, Baker Books a division of Baker Book House Company, P.O. Box 6287, Grand Rapids, MI 49516-6287, USA, ISBN 0 8010-6435-X and Inter-Varsity Press, 38, De Montfort Street, Leicester, LE1 7GP England, ISBN 0 85111-997-2

12. "Five English Reformers", J.C. Ryle, The Banner of Truth Trust, 3, Murrayfield Road, Edinburgh, EH12 6EL, P.O. Box 621, Carlisle, Pennsylvania, 17013, USA, ISBN 0 85151 138 4

13. "A Son is Given – Christ in Isaiah", Harry Uprichard, Evangelical Press, 12, Wooler Street, Darlington, Co. Durham, DL1 1RQ, England, ISBN 0 85234 301 9

14. "A Son is Promised – Christ in the Psalms", Harry Uprichard, Evangelical Press, 12, Wooler Street, Darlington, Co. Durham, DL1 1RQ, England, ISBN 085234 327 2

15. "A Son is Revealed – Discovering Christ in the Gospel of Mark", Harry Uprichard, Evangelical Press, 12, Wooler Street, Darlington, Co. Durham, DL1 1RQ, England, ISBN 0 85234 418 X

16. "An EP Study Commentary on Ephesians", Harry Uprichard, Evangelical Press, Faverdale North Industrial Estate, Darlington, Co. Durham, DL3 0PH, England, ISBN 0 85234 552 6

17. "The Apostolic Church", Thomas Witherow Free Presbyterian Publications, 133, Woodlands Road, Glasgow, G3 6LE, ISBN 0 902506 04 8

The above books may be purchased from most book sellers.